Guide to

Nantucket

Praise for previous editions:

"A new and revised edition of an old classic—the standard guide for anyone planning a trip to Nantucket."
—*Erie* (PA) *Times-News*

"This well-written book offers a wealth of information about the island . . . from transportation to restaurants, from dress codes to historic sites, from leisure activities to special events. It is thorough and helpful, and no visitor should venture there without it."
—*Springfield* (MA) *Sunday Republican*

"A practical view of this 'little gray lady,' as Nantucket was called by the nineteenth-century whalers. Historical and architectural notes will enhance your island exploration."
—*Country Living*

"The Nantucket-bound vacationer will find a wealth of information on everything from places to stay and eat to attractions such as a whaling museum, historic old homes, lighthouses, and beach areas."
—*The Midwest Book Review*

"Anyone cruising into Nantucket, or coming as a non-nautical vacationer should find this guide extremely helpful. Actually, anyone with an interest in this distinctive island will enjoy the pictures and bits of history and local lore worked into the practical information covering restaurants, hotels, transportation, tours and special events."
—*Yachting* magazine

The prices and rates listed in this guidebook were confirmed to be accurate at press time. We recommend, however, that you call establishments before traveling in order to get the most up-to-date information.

All selections of lodgings and restaurants have been made by the author. No one has paid or is paid to be in this book.

Cover photo by Cary Hazlegrove
Cover design by Saralyn D'Amato-Twomey
Text design by Deborah Nicolais

Library of Congress Cataloging-in-Publication Data
Burroughs, Polly.
    Guide to Nantucket / by Polly Burroughs. — 8th ed.
        p.   cm.
    Includes index.
    ISBN 0-7627-0412-8
    1. Nantucket Island (Mass.) — Guidebooks.   I. Title.
F72.N2B94   1999
917.44'970443—dc21   98-32211
                                                                    CIP

Manufactured in the United States of America
Eighth Edition/Second Printing

GUIDE TO
NANTUCKET

Eighth Edition

by
Polly Burroughs

The Globe Pequot Press

Guilford, Connecticut

EXPERIENCE THE WONDER OF FOXWOODS

Nestled in the beautiful New England countryside, you'll find the world's favorite casino. Foxwoods Resort Casino, now even more breathtaking than ever. Inside our magnificent new Grand Pequot Tower, you'll find a world class hotel, with 800 luxurious rooms and suites. With gourmet restaurants, and more table games, slot machines and chances to win.

Our new hotel is the perfect complement to our 312-room AAA rated four diamond Great Cedar Hotel, and our quaint Two Trees Inn, with 280 charming rooms.

Foxwoods is fine dining with 24 fabulous restaurants. And room service is available 24 hours a day, for your convenience. Foxwoods is five different gaming envi-ronments, with over 5,750 Slot Machines, Blackjack, Craps, Roulette and Baccarat, including a Smoke-Free casino.

Foxwoods is High Stakes Bingo, Keno, a Poker Room and the Ultimate Race Book.

Foxwoods is entertainment. With stars like Aretha Franklin, Engelbert Humperdinck, Paul Anka and Bill Cosby. It's two challenging golf courses. It's Championship Boxing. It's Cinetropolis, with the 1,500-seat Fox Theater. It's a Turbo Ride, Cinedrome, and our Dance Club. With its Hotels, Restaurants, Gaming and Entertainment, it's no wonder that Foxwoods has become the hottest enter-tainment destination in the country.

EXPERIENCE THE WONDER OF THE CONNECTICUT WOODS.

Conveniently located in Mashantucket. Exit 92 off I-95 in southeastern CT.

Call 1-800-PLAY-BIG

Visit our website at www.foxwoods.com

Mashantucket Pequot Tribal Nation

Contents

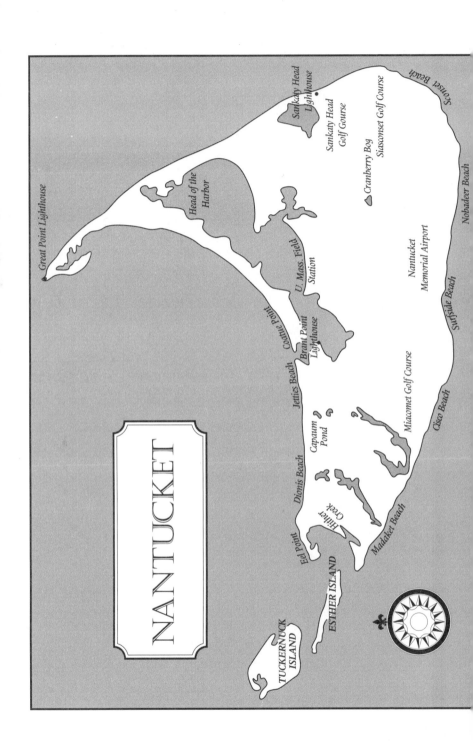

Do's and Don'ts

DO watch out on the one-way streets in town. Most of them were laid out in the eighteenth century and they are narrow, are sometimes bumpy, and have high curbstones.

DO obtain a permit from the Fire Department before you have a cookout on the beach or in your backyard.

DO keep your dog on a leash at all times when in public.

DO obtain a permit from the Nantucket Conservation Foundation before taking your four-wheel-drive vehicle out to the Coatue Wildlife Refuge, Coskata-Coatue Wildlife Refuge, or the National Wildlife Refuge at Great Point.

DO keep your voice down in the town during the evenings. No shouting.

DO dress properly when you walk in the woods, fields, or tall beach grass to avoid getting bitten by the ticks that cause Lyme Disease. It can be a very serious illness, so wear light-colored slacks and tuck the bottoms into socks. The Lyme Disease tick is the size of a sesame seed and can be seen on light-colored clothing.

DO pay attention to warnings about heavy surf and rip tides in certain areas.

DO check with the chamber of commerce if you need help with English-language translation.

DO note a restaurant's preferred type of dress for men and women at dinner.

DON'T bring your car to the island unless it's absolutely necessary. There is ample shuttle bus service to 'Sconset, Madaket, and other areas closer to town from June through September, for a very minimum charge.

DON'T plan to bring a camper to the island. There are no public campsites or trailer parks on Nantucket. Sleeping in an automobile, trailer, or camper anywhere on the island or sleeping on the beaches is illegal. Violators will be fined $200 per day.

DON'T go barefoot in town. You will not be welcome in shops or public buildings, and the Board of Health has banned bare feet in all food establishments.

DON'T wear beach attire in the center of town. Swimwear is not considered the proper attire when shopping.

DON'T drive a moped, motor scooter, or motorcycle in the Old Historic District between the hours of 10:00 P.M. and 8:00 A.M. All moped operators must wear helmets.

DON'T litter the streets, beaches, or roadways with trash of any kind. Plastic rings from six-packs kill innumerable animals, fish, and birds each year in America. Please take care!

DON'T drive on the town-owned portions of Cliffside, Dionis, Surfside, Madaket, and Jetties beaches. They are closed to all vehicles from June 1 to September 15. There is a $200 fine for all violators. A permit is required for over-sand vehicles.

DON'T plan to use any boat, barge, or raft for a residence in Nantucket Harbor or Madaket Harbor or any of their creeks or estuaries without first obtaining a permit from the Board of Health. There is a fine of $50 per day for violators.

DON'T pick any wildflowers. Many plants will die if their flowers are picked.

DON'T disturb any small clams, scallops, or other shellfish.

DON'T, under any circumstances, throw garbage or pump out holding tanks into the harbor. There are several pump-out facilities available.

DON'T bicycle on the sidewalks or the wrong way on one-way streets. No mopeds, skateboarders, or rollerblades allowed in the center of town. Observe mountain bike rules and stay on established trails.

THE
ISLAND'S
SEASONS

An old, old sight, and yet somehow so young; aye, and not changed a wink since I first saw it, a boy, from the sand-hills of Nantucket! The same!—The same!

—Herman Melville, *Moby Dick*

Thirty miles at sea from the south shore of Cape Cod, Massachusetts, lies the island of Nantucket, which in Indian tongue means "land far out at sea" or "that far-away isle." Approximately 14 miles long and 3½ miles wide at its broadest point, this "little grey lady," as it was called by the whalers in the nineteenth century, is one of the most enchanting, architecturally unique spots in America. Its shape, like that of a huge whale flipping its tail, plus its simple beauty symbolize the Island's heritage—whaling and Quakerism.

This gray-green jewel with low, rolling moors and 55 miles of sandy beaches is surrounded by the sapphire blues of Nantucket Sound and the Atlantic Ocean, whose continually shifting sands have shaped and reshaped its contours. And for more than three centuries, the sea, the wind, and the tide have molded her human history as well. It was the ocean that spawned Nantucket's great era of wealth from whaling and made possible the exquisite architecture of the historic houses. It is the ocean today that brings the Island its wealth from tourism.

With one port of entry, the town of Nantucket is a perfectly preserved New England seaport containing hundreds of authentic eighteenth- and nineteenth-century homes, unlike any other place in America. The town has cobblestone streets winding their way down to the waterfront, brick sidewalks lined with handsome wineglass elms, and electrified reproductions of old gaslights. The historic houses are close together in the English tradition, with their fences giving a continuity of line. Their old-fashioned gardens are edged with English boxwood, and roses cover the white picket and handsome wrought-iron fences.

Strolling along these narrow streets and twisting lanes on a quiet fall evening, with the whiff of wood smoke tingeing the salt air, it is just as if one had stepped back a century in time or stumbled onto a movie set for a nineteenth-century film. Restaurants in old taverns or cellars visible from the street have fires lighted, and the flickering light from the hearth plays on the beautiful antique furnishings. The twentieth century seems to intrude only sporadically here, such as in the selections in the attractive shops and the modern yachts along the waterfront.

Beyond Nantucket town there are little pockets of settlements scattered among the low, rolling moors that stretch seaward in every direction. Weathered-grey houses, in keeping with the Island's traditions, are scattered throughout the landscape. There are vast tracts of open land, and almost a third of the Island is now protected from development due to the extraordinary efforts of private citizens and many organizations. Many varieties of birds and some wildlife may be seen in these open areas. The plant life and blankets of wildflowers are a nature lover's delight.

There are four distinct seasons on Nantucket. Each season has certain characteristics that have evolved through the Island's long and fascinating history.

Beginning in early June, tourist travel to Nantucket accelerates rapidly and the Island's population expands from approximately 7,000 year-round residents to about 40,000 summer residents, including renters, hotel guests, and homeowners. Thousands also come in on the daily cruises from Cape Cod. With more than one hundred places to stay, the town is very crowded in July, and especially so in August, and reservations are a must for anyone contemplating a visit. The swimming in Nantucket Sound or Atlantic Ocean waters is superb, and there are also fishing, golf, tennis, biking, sailing, and other sports to enjoy.

Because of the surrounding sea, which is slow to warm up

and slow to cool off, autumn lingers, often reluctant to yield to winter until after Christmas. September and October are beautiful; on those halcyon fall days a yellow haze hangs over the marshland and moors in the mornings, the middays are filled with a false warmth, and the nights are pierced with cold. The fields are ablaze with goldenrod and purple aster, flocks of migrating wildfowl and songbirds touch down to rest, Arctic birds settle in for the winter months, and boats are hauled in for winter storage. The moors are sheathed in a palette of fall colors accentuated by the vivid red of the high-bush blueberry that is everywhere.

The beaches are no longer crowded, the water is still warm, and hearty swimmers find the ocean delightful until mid-October because of the Island's proximity to the Gulf Stream. While some places do shorten their hours, most of the restaurants are open through mid-October at least; many now stay open all year. The bluefish and striped bass fishing is in its prime, and the days are still pleasant for boating, sports, and nature walks. In late fall one can see the scallopers getting their old wooden workboats ready for another season of dredging the bottom of Nantucket Harbor and out along Tuckernuck Island for scallops.

Autumn at Point Breeze Hotel's water-garden lily pond.

FREDERICK G. S. CLOW

In the springtime painters keep busy preparing for the summer tourist season.

By December the Island has returned to itself, regaining its small-town character with small-town rhythms. This quieter village life is what many year-round residents really prefer. Nantucketers put a lot of time and thought into preparing for the Yuletide, and the center of town looks like an exact replica of a nineteenth-century Christmas card. The holiday season begins with Thanksgiving weekend's Nantucket Noel followed by the annual Christmas Shoppers Stroll the next weekend. Many residents think the event has become too crowded, but it is a treat for visitors, who fill the inns and hotels for the weekend. Live Christmas trees line Main Street; mulled cider, cookies, and sherry are offered in the shops brimming with Christmas gifts; and visitors stroll around town to admire the handsome holly and evergreen decorations on the historic houses. Santa and caroling enhance the festivities until the whole town sparkles with the holiday spirit. Many of the beautiful gifts for sale were made by Nantucket craftspeople. Down on the waterfront some fishermen hoist Christmas trees to the masthead to celebrate the holidays, and there is a tour of historic homes.

Midwinter is very quiet on Nantucket, and bone-chilling winds sweep across the Island. While the winters aren't as cold as those on the mainland—they are usually comparable to those in Philadelphia or Washington—the dampness is

The Christmas stroll brightens up the winter season.

Santa Claus at the Christmas stroll.

penetrating and the days grey and bleak. Summer homes have been closed for the rest of the winter, many shops and restaurants are closed, and about half the artists and craftspeople go south to return with their work in the spring. For those who do stay, it's a busy time of painting, knitting, weaving, sewing, sculpting, and designing furniture. For the visitor there are amateur theatricals, films, swimming meets, and other sporting events at the local high school; lectures and concerts at the Harbor House; and table tennis, darts, and other indoor activities to enjoy. It's a quiet time, and Main Street is deserted in the evening. But for someone who likes to walk an empty beach, curl up with a good book by the fire in one of the lovely old inns, or spend an evening learning about the Island from a local innkeeper, it can be very enjoyable. Nantucket is well known for its fine food, and some places stay open all winter.

And out on the moors snow and ice silhouette the Island's contours with a marshmallow coating over the marshes; the Island looks very beautiful and completely different from midsummer. Occasionally there is a very severe Northeaster and the ferries don't run for a day or two. Once in a while there's a severe winter cold snap when the harbor ices up and the Coast Guard's icebreaker is needed. None of these interruptions bother the Islanders, who have coped with the vagaries of life offshore for three centuries. Economically, scalloping is the important source of winter income, and the fishermen are busy on the good days out in the harbor harvesting the delicacy to be shipped to the mainland. Don't be surprised to see a hurriedly scratched sign on a shop door that says BY CHANCE OR BY APPOINTMENT or simply GONE FISHIN'.

That sapphire-blue sea, which makes the fall so pleasant and turns a raw, pewter grey in winter, keeps spring at bay, so it comes late to the Island. The days are cool and crisp, and the white gulls soaring against the bright blue, cloudless sky that is exceptionally sharp and clear at this time of year signal the start of another season. As the days begin to get longer and warmer, the Island begins to waken to the rhythms of nature, and the pace quickens. The birds return to their nesting sites, and the shadbush and the beach plum sprinkle their delicate white blossoms across the moors. Nantucket celebrates the rites of spring with the Daffodil Festival in

The famous Starbuck houses, called The Three Bricks, line the famous cobblestones of Upper Main Street. A stroll here is enjoyable year-round.

NICOLE GRANT

April, when the roadsides, gardens, shops, and parks all burst into bloom. Many, but not all, of the Island's accommodations and restaurants are open for the festival, which has become extremely popular in recent years. There are golf, tennis, nature walks, lectures, darts, a flower show, and walking the beaches for the visitor to enjoy. Swimming is unlikely, however,

for it's not until late May or early June that a hearty swimmer might be brave enough to jump into the chilly ocean.

The smell of fresh paint and the sound of hammers in the crisp air are a familiar part of early spring on the Island. Fences and houses are spruced up, and boats are painted as Islanders ready the town for another season.

Children enjoy Nantucket's beaches in the summer.

NICOLE GRANT

A Nantucket vacation is enjoyable for all ages, but the elderly might prefer to wait until spring or mid-autumn when the large crowds are gone. It would also be difficult for the elderly to get around during the Christmas Shoppers Stroll in December when snow might be a problem. The center of town could also be difficult for the disabled to manage. The cobblestoned Main Street, with its curbs and brick paving, isn't as easy as smooth surfaces for canes and wheelchairs.

One of the questions most frequently asked by a first-time visitor to Nantucket is: "Who lives on the Island in winter, and what do they do?" Descendants of the original families are now engaged in real estate, insurance, banking, gift shops, fishing, building, and shipyard work. There is a large group of retirees who have summered here for years and now are year-round residents. Many spend a few months in the midwinter in the South. Other year-round residents are young people, many of whom spent childhood summers here and prefer the Island to urban life. Some have become extremely successful artists and craftsmen. (See Winter Activities in the Leisure Activities chapter.)

So whether you prefer midsummer with all the resort activities, the semiquiet warm fall days, the mid-winter solitude and cold, or the crisp spring days with that cool, prevailing southwest wind coming off the water, you'll find Nantucket is fascinating. This guide is designed to help you discover some of the Island's great charm whatever your means of transportation, the season of the year, or the length of your stay.

Nantucket Temperatures

For those curious about what type of clothing to bring, the average highs and lows are: January 40°F and 10°F; February 41°F and 26°F; March 42°F and 28°F; April 53°F and 40°F; May 62°F and 48°F; June 71°F and 58°F; July 78°F and 63°F; August 76°F and 61°F; September 70°F and 66°F; October 59°F and 47°F; November 48°F and 37°F; and December 40°F and 26°F.

Surf at Siasconset's Great Beach.

Nantucket Harbor looking toward Brant Point.

2

A
BRIEF
HISTORY

*And thus have these naked Nantucketers, these sea-hermits,
issuing from their anthill in the sea, overrun and conquered the
world like so many Alexanders.*

—Herman Melville, *Moby Dick*

While there are many legends about the origin of
Nantucket, the favorite involves the giant Moshup, an Indian
tutelary divinity who lived on Cape Cod. He is said to have
tossed his sand-filled moccasins out to sea one sleepless
night to create the Islands of Nantucket and Martha's
Vineyard. Another story tells of Moshup knocking the ashes
out of his pipe, which settled down on the sea to make the
Island.

Nantucket's natural formation came about during the last
Ice Age. The first mention in recorded history of this terminal
moraine of sand and gravel was made in 1602 by
Bartholomew Gosnold, the English explorer who had discovered Martha's Vineyard. He vaguely described the course of
his vessel in relation to Nantucket. But it was George
Waymouth, another Englishman, who gave the nautical position of Nantucket in 1604 and mentioned the "whitish sandy
cliffe" of Sankaty Head, although he didn't go ashore. Had he
done so, he would have seen the low moorland, long stretches
of sandy beach, huge protected harbor, ponds, kettle holes,
coves, and lagoons populated by Indians who belonged to the
Narragansett tribe of the Algonquin family.

In 1641, Thomas Mayhew of Watertown, Massachusetts,
purchased for forty pounds Martha's Vineyard, Nantucket,
and the Elizabeth Islands from two English noblemen who
held conflicting grants to these Islands. With his son, and

Sea Culture

To the old-time Nantucketers, an important person is one who "draws a lot of water." (Large vessels require much deeper water than small ones.)

Waste and extravagance is said to be "Two lamps burning and no ship at sea."

During the whaling era, it was a tradition to put a black cat under a tub or bucket the night before a ship was due to sail. This was supposed to create a head wind that would make the ship's embarkment impossible, and the wife or sweetheart would have one more day with her loved one.

others, Mayhew planned to establish a manorial system of land tenure similar to that in England and to convert the Indians to Christianity. The group settled in Edgartown on Martha's Vineyard, and its members, as well as Vineyard Indians who had been converted to Christianity, visited Nantucket from time to time, becoming acquainted with the Indians who lived there.

It was in 1659 that Tristram Coffin, a planter living in Salisbury, Massachusetts, north of Boston, surveyed Nantucket and opened negotiations to purchase it from Mayhew. Coffin and a group of friends strongly resented the rigid code of the Puritans in the Boston area and sought the freedom of their own community. Because of the untimely death of his son and consuming work on Martha's Vineyard, Mayhew agreed to sell all of Nantucket except for a small portion at Quaise. A deed was drawn up on July 2, 1659, by which Mayhew sold to the nine Salisbury purchasers his patent "for the sum of thirty pounds in good Marchantable Pay in ye Massachusetts under which government they now Inhabit . . . and two Beaver Hatts, one for myself and one for my wife."

These nine original buyers were Tristram Coffin and his son Peter, Thomas Macy, and Messrs. Folger, Swain, Hussey, Barnard, Greenleaf, and Pike. According to William Macy's *History of Nantucket,* published in 1923, each person, including Mayhew, was given a share. To encourage more people to

COURTESY OF NANTUCKET HISTORICAL ASSOCIATION

Captain Charles Myrick, *oil on canvas,*
by Eastman Johnson, 1879.
Captain Myrick, who was in the coastwise trade, was a favorite model of Eastman Johnson. Johnson was one of several well-known artists, including the American impressionist Childe Hassam, who found the light and scenery superb. The Peter Folger Research Center has two other Johnson paintings.

join the settlement, each original proprietor was granted another share to allow him to choose a partner. Then they issued fourteen half-shares to craftsmen, in return for their skills for the proposed settlement. Thus, the group became known as the twenty-seven original whole- and half-share-holders under whom all the land of the Island, except Mayhew's property at Quaise, was held in common for many

18   Guide to Nantucket years. In subsequent years the full-shareholders and half-shareholders would engage in many bitter battles to wrest political control from one another.

Thomas Macy was the first of the group to leave the mainland for Nantucket. A Baptist, he had found religious prejudice in the New World nearly as bad as it was in the Old World. He had gotten along well in the community, despite the Puritans' intolerance, and being kindhearted, he had allowed some Quakers to take refuge in his house one stormy day. This was reported to the Puritan authorities, who had been

The last male Indian on Nantucket, Abram Quary, put on a coat and cravat for this painting, although he discarded his shoes. Abram lived alone on the Island and made baskets for sale.

so distrustful of the rapidly growing Society of Friends that they passed a law making it a criminal offense for anyone to entertain Quakers. Macy was fined, and two of the men he had taken in were later hung for professing their religion. Macy needed little urging to leave, and in the fall of 1659 he made the voyage from north of Boston in an open boat with his wife, five children, a friend, Edward Starbuck, and twelve-year-old Isaac Coleman.

Their landfall, near Madaket on the western end of the Island, allowed for a quick exodus toward the Vineyard should they encounter any trouble with the Indians. The Algonquin natives, who were divided into the territories of Sachems Potconet, Autoscot, Wauwinet, and Wanackmamack, treated them kindly, however; the natives willingly shared their knowledge of how to harvest food to survive.

The sandy, gravelly soil and relentless winds were hostile to planters. One can only imagine the settlers' first lonely, bleak winter in a crudely built cabin with small children to feed and keep warm.

The following spring others began to arrive from Salisbury until, by the end of the year, there were sixty settlers in all. They settled in the area near Capaum Pond, which was a little harbor, and they called it Sherburne. By 1720 the harbor was landlocked and the residents decided to move the town to the present harbor. They continued to call it Sherburne until 1795, when they changed the name to Nantucket.

The hospitable Indians taught these new arrivals what they knew of fishing, killing wildfowl, and farming and introduced them to the Island's wild cranberries. The settlers, in turn, repurchased their tracts of land from the natives as specified by Mayhew and worked to educate the Indians. The Indians soon realized they had forfeited necessary use of their lands for grazing and other purposes and spent years, in vain, trying to reclaim them. Both the diseases of the white man and his "firewater" took their toll in the end. The last male Nantucket Indian, Abram Quary, died in 1854.

Obed Macy, in his 1843 *History of Nantucket*, laments the tragedy: "In the simple charity of nature they rescued our Fathers. When fugitives from Christian persecution they opened to them their stores, bestowed on them their lands, treated them with unfailing kindness, acknowledged their superiority, tasted their poison and died. Their only misfortune was their connection with the Christians and their only crime, their imitation of their manners."

The first group of settlers included many skilled half-shareholders—a carpenter, joiner, miller, shoemaker, tailor, farmer, seaman, and others—to make the growing community as self-sufficient as possible. They imported only those things they couldn't make or grow themselves. Sheep and cattle were introduced and grazed freely on the common lands. Farming was done on a subsistence level on very poor soil.

It was inevitable that they would turn more and more to the sea for their livelihood. Spinning and weaving had been the main occupations, but when the Wool Act of 1699 forbade the sale of wool cloth between the colonies, whaling became an economic alternative. In 1712, when Captain Christopher Hussey was blown out to sea, he came upon a school of spermaceti whales and managed to harpoon one. Until this time only right whales (so-called because they were considered the right whale to kill) were being hunted close to shore. Hussey's chance encounter set the course that was eventually to make Nantucket the whaling capital of the world. These Islanders perfected deep-sea whaling, excelling in the art of harpooning the huge mammal, sometimes 100 feet long, from a small whaleboat. Once harpooned, the whale usually sped off angrily on a perilous "Nantucket sleigh ride" through the ocean until it was worn down. Other times it knocked the whaleboat to kindling wood in a matter of seconds, or rammed the whaleship itself again and again until the vessel sank. It was an extremely dangerous business, which one whaleman said extracted "a drop of blood for every drop of oil." Whalemen endured mutiny, cannibalism, stench, suffering, and sacrifice in their global voyages, which could last years. But a "greasy" trip meant huge profits to be shared—to many, well worth the risks and hardships.

As the hunt for sperm oil grew, the Islanders began to relocate into the town above the harbor front, which was rapidly expanding with the building of warehouses, candle factories, rope walks, and other businesses related to whaling. For a century and a half, whale hunting controlled the Island's economy and the Quaker religion dictated its way of life, including the architecture. The original settlers had sought

***Captain Fred Parker,
c. 1880***
*After a life at sea,
accustomed to small
quarters and months of
solitude, some seamen
who had no families
continued a reclusive
existence when they
retired. Captain Fred
Parker was known as the
hermit of Quidnet, where
he spent his last days.*

total freedom from Puritan ways, and for fifty years after their arrival there was no formal religion of any kind, although Quaker missionaries from England often visited the Island. But in 1708 Mary Coffin Starbuck, a very strong, influential woman (the type Nantucket had to manage the home and town affairs while the men were away at sea for months at a time), became a Quaker and organized the Monthly Meeting of Friends in her home. She attracted many followers. The Quaker philosophy of pacifism, personal liberty, temperance, and hard work, as well as the belief that a spiritual intermediary was unnecessary, appealed to these independent Islanders. As whaling and the Quaker faith dominated the community, even their language became a curious mixture of Quaker and nautical expressions.

The Quakers were opposed to slavery, so by the 1770s there were only a few slaves on the Island. One was named Boston, who was owned by William Swain. On Boston's return from a whaling voyage aboard the Friendship, the Swains claimed Boston's share of the profits should go to them. William Rotch, one of the most prominent and successful Islanders at the time, owned the Friendship and was not going to tolerate this injustice. He went to court, defending Boston, and won his case, striking the first blow for emancipation of blacks in the state a century before the Civil War. Soon after that there were no more slaves on the Island.

Also living on the Island were Portuguese blacks who had been recruited as crewmen on whaleships that had stopped in the Cape Verde Islands off the coast of Africa. By 1820 there were 275 blacks listed in the Nantucket census of 7,300 residents. Most of them lived on upper Pleasant Street, which was known as "New Guinea."

The blacks were excellent crewmen, for the most part, and there were many in the crew aboard the whaleship Brothers when it was trapped by a storm off the coast of New Zealand. With the stern to the rocky shore and an impossible head wind, Captain Benjamin Worth met with his officers to consider whether they should continue to try to get the vessel out of there or run it aground. Word spread quickly through the vessel, and the sailors went to Captain Worth and begged him to try once more. They had heard many stories of cannibalism about this part of New Zealand. The captain agreed to try one more time, and fortunately the weather broke and the whaleship escaped.

Cannibalism was such a part of life in the Pacific during those early years that William Endicott in his 1820s journal described the Fiji Islanders' method of cooking bodies, similar to a clambake. A hole was dug in the sand, hot coals were spread out, wet leaves and layers of flesh were put in with old mats spread over them to confine the steam, and "in twenty minutes the flesh was cooked."

Yet not all South Sea Islanders were hostile. Hawaiian women adored the Nantucket sailors and would swim naked out to the whaleships when they sailed into port. A whaling captain was not averse to reminding a restless and difficult crew after many monotonous months at sea that in no time they would be in the Hawaiian Islands.

A Quaker whaling wife was so overwhelmed by the lush beauty and flowers of Hawaii, compared to Nantucket's winter, that she wrote home, "I thought I had died and gone to heaven."

During the last part of the eighteenth century, Nantucketers were carrying on a very lucrative trade with England, shipping oil, ambergris, and candles to London. (In fact, it was the crime in the streets of London that helped the Nantucket economy as much as anything, for the Londoners put oil lamps on the streets to try to improve the situation.) Things were going very well indeed until 1773, when three Nantucket ships, *Beaver, Dartmouth,* and *Bedford,* having taken cargoes of oil and candles to London, returned to Boston loaded with tea, which was thrown overboard to protest a British tax during the famous Boston Tea Party.

As the Revolutionary War gained momentum, residents of Nantucket tried to remain neutral because the Quakers were pacifists and also economically dependent on England, where they had many social and blood ties. At the same time, they were fiercely independent, proud to be Americans, and geographically in an impossible position where they were vulnerable on both sides. Finally, a large number of Islanders rallied to their country's cause and served on American ships, but they paid a heavy price. When they returned home after the war, they were disowned by the Quakers. Having been distrusted by both sides in the war, the Islanders suffered heavy losses from both the Americans and the British.

After the war, recovery was slow and many impoverished citizens really suffered, while others left the Island. But the whaling fleet was gradually rebuilt, and when the whaleship *Beaver* rounded the Horn in 1791 and opened the Pacific to whaling, Nantucket's industry prospered once again. Nantucket whalemen lived on the Pacific for months on end, more familiar with the Fiji Islands or Hawaii than Nantucket, where they spent only a brief time with their families. They had to rely on their strong and capable Quaker women, dressed in coal-scuttle bonnets, long homespun dresses, and shawls, to manage the children, run their homes, and tend to many of the town's affairs.

This prosperity was short-lived, however; it ended with the outbreak of the War of 1812. Nantucket's fleet numbered 116 vessels, and with the memory of the Revolution still fresh in their minds, Nantucketers were horrified to be in the middle of another war. They were defenseless, and the Quakers were pacifists, determined to take no active part in the war. The Islanders tried to keep on good terms with both sides, with the natural result that they were trusted by neither. Ships were seized by both the British and French navies, and the Island was blockaded. Losses were severe, leaving only twenty-three vessels in the fleet. For about three years Nantucket was in a severely depressed state, as it had been after the Revolution, but gradually the fleet was built up once again. With the discovery of the lucrative Japanese whaling grounds after the war, Nantucket forged into its golden era.

The harbor was jammed with whaleships; some fitting out for another long voyage, others unloading their barrels of oil and rolling them into one of the large warehouses. Not only were casks of oil exported to light the lamps of half the world's capitals at that time, but also whalebone for ladies' corsets, candles made at the twenty-four candle factories in town, and precious ambergris, used for perfume and fine soap, were shipped to England, France, and other countries. The harbor front was crowded with industries related to whaling: sail lofts, shipyards, blacksmith shops fashioning razor-sharp harpoons and lances, rope walks, cooperages making barrels for oil, and bakeries making hardtack for the long voyages of these "blubber hunters."

It was during this period of enormous prosperity, when every whaleman worked on a "lay" system whereby profits from these successful voyages were shared, that Nantucket's stately mansions on Upper Main Street were built by the merchants who owned the whaleships. (The whaling captains, who endured all the hardships, lived in houses such as those on Orange Street, where a hundred captains were supposed to have lived at one time.) The building boom quickly used up the large trees on the Island, and lumber had to be imported. Henry David Thoreau wrote in 1854, "There is not a tree to be seen except such as are set about houses." Herman Melville, author of *Moby Dick,* called it an "elbow of sand" and quipped that "pieces of wood in Nantucket are carried about like bits of the true cross in Rome"; that people there "plant toadstools before their houses to get under the shade in the summertime." The shipowners' houses were furnished with precious silks, Indian rugs, Oriental porcelains, Chinese furniture, and other elegant furnishings from what became known as the China Trade. Concerts, lectures, and other cultural activities flourished during this period of great affluence, while the Quaker traditions of simplicity slowly diminished.

Old 'Sconset Pump was the primary source of drinking water from 1776 until the early 1900s.

These whaling voyages, which lasted up to three years, required large vessels that drew so much water they were unable to get over the shoals marking the entrance to Nantucket Harbor. Although a "camel," or dry-dock arrangement, was built to lift them over the bar, it proved unworkable. The ships were soon obliged to fit out at Edgartown on Martha's Vineyard or New Bedford, which eventually became the whaling capital of America.

Nantucket was still at the peak of her whaling days when a fire broke out on Main Street in 1838, destroying some of the buildings. It was followed eight years later by the fire of 1846 that completely gutted the center of the town, burning more than 300 buildings. All the businesses along the waterfront that were connected with the whaling industry went up in flames. As the town struggled to rebuild after this devastation, word of the California Gold Rush spread through the maritime community. As a result, many Nantucket seamen jumped ship in California eager to join the march to the gold-fields. Nantucket whaling masters had difficulty shipping competent crews. With the Island's economy in such dire straits, it's surprising that Nantucketers put so much thought into rebuilding after the fire. The buildings on the Main Street square were well built, and the cobblestone street was widened to prevent another similar catastrophe.

But the discovery of petroleum in 1859, followed by the Civil War, during which the whaling fleet was virtually destroyed, dealt the final, fatal blow to Nantucket's industry. In a few short years, her two-centuries-old economy was dead.

While the rest of New England entered into the Industrial Revolution following the Civil War, Nantucket lay dormant. Many of the houses were shuttered and abandoned, deteriorating from neglect. Docks were crumbling and grass grew between the cobblestones on the side streets. Some houses were moved off-Island on coastwise schooners, those broad-beamed, gaff-rigged vessels used to move freight under canvas all along the eastern seaboard.

The remaining inhabitants, with stalwart determination and reserve, earned a living from commercial fishing, shell-fishing, harvesting cranberries, and some sheep husbandry.

Attempts at industrializing Nantucket failed, sparing the Island unsightly mills and adjacent slums, as well as much Victorian architecture. These were harsh times, but gradually another business began to emerge that would eventually become the Island's economic salvation.

Beginning in the mid-nineteenth century, saltwater bathing became the rage for vacationers who previously had enjoyed the supposed therapeutic value of mountain watering places with mineral springs. Hotels and rooming houses began to spring up on the Island in the 1840s, in the town of Nantucket as well as in the outlying village of Siasconset. The first newspaper advertisement for a cottage to rent ran in 1865. Tourism was just a trickle at first, but in 1870 when steamboat service from New Bedford to Nantucket began, the Massachusetts Old Colony Railroad started promoting vacation travel. In 1872 fishing for bluefish became another attraction for summer visitors. Tourism soon flourished and grew until it became the Island's primary business.

That long impoverished period, that pause when history lay dormant in the dark and empty houses, became, in the long run, Nantucket's most valuable asset. By losing its economy and being relatively isolated as an island, Nantucket preserved its character. By the time it became a well-known resort, the newcomers who bought and restored the houses found this perfectly preserved heritage from the eighteenth and nineteenth centuries to be priceless. The new structures blend in quietly and unobtrusively because of the rigid design controls that have been in place for years.

Paul Goldberger, architecture critic of the *New York Times,* has noted of Nantucket, "It is one of the East Coast's most exhilarating ocean landscapes, and its harborside town is still arguably the most beautiful eighteenth- and nineteenth-century village in the country. Nantucket is a real town, not a suburb; it emanates urbanity as decisively as Boston, and this is crucial to the Island's magic."

A View of Nantucket Town from Straight Wharf.

3

How to Get There

Nantucket! Take out your map and look at it. See what a real corner of the world it occupies; how it stands there, away offshore . . . a mere hillock, and elbow of sand; all beach without a background.

—Herman Melville, *Moby Dick*

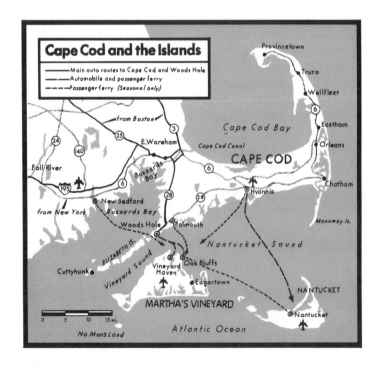

Because Nantucket is an island, getting there takes a little more planning than just getting in a car, but there is always a certain excitement about an island vacation. The only public means of reaching the Island are by air or by the ferries that leave the Cape Cod town of Hyannis. The town of Hyannis, located midway along the south shore of Cape Cod, is about a forty-five–minute drive from the entrance to the Cape. This drive can take considerably longer during the summer, especially on weekends. Hyannis is about 80 miles from Boston, 165 miles from Hartford, 270 miles from New York, and 500 miles from Washington D.C.

Car

Driving from Boston to Hyannis takes about two hours, but you should allow more time in the heavy summer traffic. From downtown Boston take the Southeast Expressway (Route 3) to the Sagamore Bridge over the Cape Cod Canal. Take the Mid-Cape Highway (Route 6) to Route 132, which leads on down to Hyannis.

Driving from New York City may take six hours or more in traffic. Take Interstate 95 North to Providence, Rhode Island; then take Route 195 East to the Cape Cod Canal at the Bourne Bridge. Follow along on either side of the canal to the Sagamore Bridge and the Mid-Cape Highway (Route 6). Turn off the Mid-Cape Highway at Route 132 and follow the signs to Hyannis. Allow ample time if you're leaving your car on the Cape in the Hy-Line or Steamship Authority parking lot, which charges $7.50 per day (and is subject to increase).

Train and Bus

Bonanza Bus Lines provides bus service from Providence (888–751–8800) and from the Port Authority Building in New York City (212–947–1766) to Hyannis.

Off from On

An off-islander or visitor has been called a "coof," probably from the Scotch word meaning "fool" or "simpleton." If someone says they're "off from on," it means an Island resident has temporarily gone off-island to the mainland, which many Nantucketers refer to as America.

The Plymouth and Brockton Company provides bus service between Hyannis and Boston, including Logan Airport. Call (508) 778–9767 or (508) 775–6502.

Plymouth and Brockton bus company also has a bus service that connects Kingston, the last stop on Boston's South Shore commuter rail with the Hyannis ferry dock. Travelers bound for Nantucket will change buses at the Sagamore bus lot. One-way fare, which includes both bus and ferry tickets, is $12.00.

Ferry

Once you've arrived in Hyannis, you have two choices of ships—the Steamship Authority and the Hy-Line company—to take you over to Nantucket. Choose the ship you'll take according to your need for your car on the Island; only the Steamship Authority allows cars on its ferries.

Newcomers to the Island frequently ask, "Should I bring my car?" The chamber of commerce, selectmen, and other town officials urge you not to bring your automobile if your visit is short and you are staying in the town of Nantucket itself. The Main Street area becomes extremely congested in July and August; with the availability of taxis and buses, or rental bikes, mopeds, and cars, you will find it much more convenient not to have an automobile to worry about. However, if your stay is for a week or more or you are planning to be in outlying areas on the Island such as Siasconset, Wauwinet, or Madaket, you will want your car.

The Woods Hole, Martha's Vineyard, and Nantucket Steamship Authority operates daily ferries from Hyannis to Nantucket, carrying passengers as well as cars and trucks. It is a two-and-one-quarter-hour trip from Hyannis. During the summer, there are six regularly scheduled ferry departures daily from the dock in Hyannis. From early fall through late spring, the ferry schedule is quite different, so always call ahead to determine current schedules (508–228–3274), reservations (508–477–8600).

Remember there is no standby on weekends or three-day holiday weekends.

Reservations for bringing automobiles on and off the Island must be made weeks or months in advance by phoning the Steamship Authority's office, but passengers do not need reservations. Always allow ample time to get to the ferry. (You must be at the dock at least thirty minutes prior to sailing time if you have a car reservation.) If you decide to leave your car on the mainland, give yourself plenty of time to find a parking place. It costs $7.50 per day to park in the Authority's parking lot ($6.00 off-season). The Hy-Line's parking lot is also nearby.

Transportation costs on the Authority's ferries from Hyannis are as follows, but they are subject to rate increase:

Round-trip automobile fare
(May 15–October 14) $202.00
Early spring and late fall 144.00
Winter 110.00
Adult passenger one-way fare 11.00
Child (5–12) one-way fare 5.50
Bicycle one-way fare 5.50

For handicapped access, please contact the terminal agent or the ferry's purser.

The Hy-Line ferries carry only passengers and bicycles from its Ocean Street dock in Hyannis from May through October, and one runs year-round. No reservations are necessary. For the ferry schedule, call the Hyannis office (888–778–1132) or the Nantucket office (508–228–3949). Rates are $11.00 for adults one way, $5.50 for children three to twelve years old, and $4.50 for bicycles. First class, one way,

Many Nantucket visitors come to the island on their own boats.

$20.00. Adult one-way fare is $11.00, children five to twelve are $5.00, four and under free.

Hy-Line now has year-round service; a new catamaran, *M. V. Grey Lady,* which makes six trips a day (May–October); and fewer daily trips off-season. For advance reservations on any ferries call (508) 778–1602.

Hy-Line also runs a boat from Martha's Vineyard to Nantucket, and another "Around the Sound" cruise. This one leaves Hyannis in the early morning, spends three hours in Nantucket, three hours in Martha's Vineyard, returning to Hyannis at 9:30 P.M. Fares for adults round-trip, $33.00, children twelve and under $16.50, children under four are free. Parking for all Hy-Line boats is $9.00 per day.

During the midsummer, the Authority ferry and the Hy-Line boats may be loaded to capacity. You may telephone the Hy-Line a day ahead for first-class passenger reservations. Or, if you find one ferry is filled, you can easily walk over to the other wharf to check on the other company's ship.

Private Boat

If you own a boat and plan to cruise on it to Nantucket, call ahead to make a reservation for a slip or a mooring. These are difficult to obtain during the summer, so it's advisable to call as far in advance as possible.

The slips at the Nantucket Boat Basin have phone jacks, showers, electricity, and a laundromat for the boat owners. For further details, call the Harbormaster (508–228–7260). Nantucket Moorings (508–228–4472) has moorings to rent by the day. Launch service in the harbor is provided by Harbor Launch, Straight Wharf (508–228–8565), and by Nantucket Yacht Club (for members and guests only). If you need to reach the Nantucket marine operator, call (205) 393–9335. (For VHF marine calls, dial the operator and ask for the Nantucket marine operator.) Madaket Marine (508–228–9086) also has moorings.

Plane

The other way to get to Nantucket is by plane. There are several airlines with direct flights to the Island from Northeast cities, or you can drive part of the way to the Island and fly the rest of the way.

It is becoming increasingly popular for people coming from New York, New Jersey, and points south to fly from New Bedford, Massachusetts, directly to the Island. This avoids all the Cape Cod traffic, saving one and a half hours of driving time. Parking fee is $5.00 per day in the summer. No fee off-season. Plane fare costs $64 one way in season; $49 fall through spring. Parking is free at the New Bedford airport, and there are several flights a day during the summer.

Another alternative is to fly from Hyannis. There are many flights during the summer. From the late fall until spring, all the airlines sharply reduce the number of flights.

The airline companies flying planes in and out of Nantucket seem to change quite often, and schedules change from season to season. It's a very busy airport with private planes, charter flights, and ample flights by the various lines in the summer months and limited service off-season. It is best to check with your travel agent, the Nantucket Chamber of Commerce (508–228–1700), or the Nantucket Information Bureau (508–228–0925). There are always flights available from Boston; New York City; New Bedford, Massachusetts; Hyannis; Martha's Vineyard Island; Providence, Rhode Island; and Newark, New Jersey.

Because of the many variables in the airlines serving the Island and the prices, it is best to check this information with your travel bureau or the chamber of commerce.

For those flying in their own planes, Nantucket Memorial Airport is tower controlled between 0600 and 2100. Runway 6-24 (6,300 feet long) has an instrument landing system. Fuel is available twenty-four hours daily (100 LL, Jet A). Overnight parking and tie-downs as well as aircraft repair and servicing facilities are available. The airport tower is (508) 228–0464; operations is (508) 325–5307.

Whether you take a plane or boat to the Island, you'll find the trip a memorable experience. From the air, the sculptured blues and greens of the sea and the meandering, sandy shoals

The M.V. Grey Lady, *Hy-Line's new year-round water jet Catamaran, travels from Hyannis to Nantucket in one hour.*

NICOLE GRANT

dotted with white sails are a beautiful sight. Those long stretches of white, sandy beaches and clear water look very inviting.

The ferry ride is equally delightful, perhaps even more so for the newcomer, for it is a unique way of becoming acquainted with other islands as you approach Nantucket. A favorite pastime is tossing bits of food to the sea gulls that swoop and dive overhead as they follow the ferries.

As the ferry cruises down Nantucket Sound, the large island on the starboard side of the vessel (your right) is Martha's Vineyard. This island is twice the size of Nantucket and has become an equally popular summer resort. The last easily identifiable point is the lighthouse at Cape Pogue on

An idyllic scene out on Coatue.

Chappaquiddick Island, which is part of Martha's Vineyard. As the Island passes from view, the ferry continues out into Nantucket Sound toward the Gulf Stream, which is responsible for Nantucket's mild climate and warm water. In fact, it was Benjamin Franklin who, with the help of a whaling captain cousin, first charted the Gulf Stream in 1769. Franklin's grandparents, Peter and Mary Morrill Folger, were members of Nantucket's founding families, and his mother, Abiah, was born and raised on the Island.

As the ferry approaches Nantucket, the sea's colorful collage of blues and greens is deceptive. The waters in places are extremely shallow, and with the strong currents that swirl around the Island, this has been one of the worst graveyards for ships on the eastern seaboard. A New Bedford newspaper once estimated that between 1843 and 1903, more than 2,100 vessels had been wrecked on Nantucket shoals alone!

The first sight of land, a low, purplish streak on the horizon on your right, is the deserted, privately owned Muskeget Island, home to a colony of gray seals. Coming into view to the left of Muskeget is the sparsely settled Tuckernuck Island, also privately owned. As the ferry moves on, Great Point, the narrow, northern tip of Nantucket, becomes visible off the ferry's port bow, while the sandy cliffs off the starboard bow are the Dionis Beach area. The Great Point Lighthouse is a replica of the original, which guided ships for 166 years before it was claimed by the sea in a fierce winter storm in 1984. The replacement was built in 1986.

A blinker marks the entrance to the jetties that protect the channel into Nantucket Harbor. The land on your left is Coatue, a long, narrow, scalloped barrier beach known for its acres of beach roses, prickly pear cactus, and cedar trees sculpted close to the ground by the prevailing southwest winds. This area is best seen from the ferry and can be reached only by boat or by jeep from Wauwinet. The ferry slips between the jetties, rounds the famous Brant Point light, and cruises on into the wharf.

Stepping ashore is like strolling into the mid-nineteenth century, when sailors, carrying their ditty bags and luggage thrown over their shoulders, trudged up the cobblestone streets to their lodgings. Many visitors, with baggage trailing, walk to their inn or hotel. With the streets lined with historic nineteenth-century mansions, and charming eighteenth-century houses on the narrow, winding lanes, the town itself is not a reproduction of an earlier era, but completely authentic. It is overflowing with lovely gardens, and colorful window boxes and the ingenious use of space create tiny and large courtyards for outside dining and add to the allure for which the town is noted. This extraordinary setting, interrupted only by the necessary twentieth-century amenities, is a treasure.

4

HOW TO GET AROUND

It is not essential to have your own car to enjoy the island. At the wharves as well as at the airport, taxis, buses, bicycles, mopeds, and cars are available for transportation.

Taxis

There are quite a few taxi companies on Nantucket. Some operate only in season, while others are open year-round. The yellow pages of the phone book list them all. Most taxis also offer tours.

A taxi ride from the airport, which is 2½ miles from town, costs $7.00 for one passenger and $1.00 for each additional passenger. From the center of town it costs $10.00 to Cisco and Quaise; $12.00 to Madaket, Siasconset, Quidnet, and Pocomo; These prices are subject to change and all are based on mileage.

On-Island Transportation

Nantucket now provides shuttle bus transportation daily to Siasconset via Polpis Road and via Old South Road, Madaket, the South Loop, and Miacomet Loop. For sightseeing, tour buses are available by the hour at Barrett's, Grimes, Nantucket Island Tours, and All Point. Automobile rentals are available at the airport and in town. Young's, which has been in business for sixty-five years, has cars, jeeps, bikes, and mopeds. Cook's, Holiday Cycle, and Nantucket Bike Shop also have bikes, mopeds, and scooters. Hertz, Thrifty, Budget, Nantucket Windmill, and others provide different types of cars, jeeps, and minibuses.

If you come to the Island during the summer, especially in August when it is most crowded, it is advisable to rent your

Harvey Young, owner of Young's Bicycle Shop, on his favorite bike.

bicycle, moped, or car in advance. Be aware, however, that the main part of town during the summer becomes extremely congested, and a car here becomes a nuisance.

Nantucket lends itself to bicycling, as it is relatively flat and most areas are within easy reach. There are bicycle paths from town out to Surfside, Madaket, and Siasconset, and bicyclists must use them instead of the roads. Riders of bikes and mopeds are cautioned to pay close attention to Nantucket's rules and regulations, and violators now receive tickets.

Mopeds may not be used on bike paths, one-way street signs should be observed, and no bike riding is allowed on sidewalks. If you are riding after dark, the law requires front and rear reflectors, and it is also advisable to have a light. Mopeds and motorcycles are prohibited in the Old Historic District between 10:00 P.M. and 8:00 A.M. Both Main and Liberty streets are cobblestone and impossible to bike, so it's best to use the nearby parallel streets. Riding on sand tracks and dirt roads is extremely hazardous; there have been many accidents. Watch for any new bike paths.

Distances from town to the outlying areas are:

Airport	2½ miles
Cisco	4½ miles
Dionis Beach	2½ miles
Jetties Beach	1 mile
Life Saving Museum	2½ miles
Madaket	5½ miles
Polpis	6 miles
Quaise	4 miles
Quidnet	7 miles
Siasconset	9 miles
Surfside	2½ miles
Wauwinet	5½ miles

Vintage car, Nantucket.

AROUND THE HORN PITCAIRN 14,300 MI.
N.ZEALAND 15,800 MI.
SAMOA 15,000 MI.
TAHITI 14,650 MI.
VALPARAISO 5,335 MILES
MELBOURNE 11,253 MILES
DAYTONA BEACH 1,282 MILES
BUENOS AYRES 6,914 MILES
SCONSET 7½ MILES

20 MILES

NANTUCKET LOOMS

MACKIN

ICELA
POLE

BERMUDA 690 MI.

HALIFAX 48   ILES
CAPE VERDE ISL
BERLIN 4,185 MI.   200 MI.

BOMBAY 9,554 MI.
ROME 4,654 MI.

CALCU

The world in relation to Nantucket—artists spruce up the sign on Washington Street.

5

WHERE TO STAY

If you are planning a visit to Nantucket, the earlier you make your reservations the better; January is not too soon. If you wait until spring, chances are you may not be able to find any housekeeping units, particularly for August, and the best hotel suites and cottages may have been reserved.

With tourism the source of Nantucket's economy today, the Island has many possible accommodations for visitors— hotels, inns, apartments, private guest houses, and small rental cottages. There are also houses available for rent. There are not, however, any public or private campgrounds, and camping of any sort is prohibited on the Island.

Visitors who want to pay by the night for an accommodation should stay at a hotel, inn, private guest house, or bed-and-breakfast. These are available in a wide price range. For instance, some Nantucket accommodations are on the European Plan (EP), which means rooms without meals; some are on the Modified American Plan (MAP), which provides room, dinner, and breakfast; others provide room and continental breakfast. Most places require a minimum stay of two nights.

The bed and breakfasts and private guest houses do not lend themselves to small, active children. Most of them were formerly private homes and are furnished with antiques. The hotels or other places that are on the beaches or that provide lawn areas and swimming pools for children to romp in are much more relaxing for families.

Visitors staying at least one week will probably choose an apartment or cottage. Apartments, usually consisting of bedroom, living room, and kitchenette, are available in some of the guest houses as well as the hotels. Short-term rental cottages are usually very small and simple and may be part of a hotel complex or a cottage community.

Generally the rates for bed and breakfasts range from $75

to $150 per couple per night in season (June 15 to October 15). Rooms and suites in the inns and hotels range in price from $70 to $400 per couple per day. Cottage and apartment rental rates vary depending on location, type, and size. Typical rates are from about $150 per day for one bedroom and from about $300 per day for two bedrooms. Spring and fall rates for all accommodations are usually 10 percent or sometimes 20 percent less, and off-season rates, November to April, are usually half-price, except for the Christmas Stroll.

Private homes are available for rent through Nantucket real estate offices. Prices for monthly or seasonal rentals range from a few thousand dollars to $50,000 or more for a large house.

There are several accommodations services on the Island that can be most helpful to visitors looking for a place to stay. Most places don't allow pets and require a minimum stay of two nights and a deposit of half or all of the cost for your stay.

Nantucket Accommodations is a reservations service that lists many, but not all, of the guest houses and hotels on the Island. They will describe the facilities to you over the telephone and make a booking for you. They are at 4 Dennis Drive, and their phone number is (508) 228–9559.

Nantucket Vacation Rentals, on Ash Lane, is a service listing some cottages, apartments, and houses to rent. Call them at (508) 228–3131 for more information.

Nantucket Information Bureau is a town-operated information bureau that puts out a detailed brochure on everything from places to stay to car rentals. They will not make reservations for you, but they do keep track of hotel vacancies (from day to day only). They are at 25 Federal Street, and their phone number is (508) 228–0925.

If you're planning a visit in the spring or fall, be sure to bring both summer and light woolen clothing. The weather can be very changeable during these seasons. The fall, however, is pretty certain to stay warm because of the surrounding ocean, which is slow to cool off. A very light coat or sweater will be needed in the evening any time from May to October.

The following accommodations are just a small sampling of the many delightful places to stay on Nantucket. The letter "C" is used in headings to indicate lodgings especially appropriate for children. It's best to ask if there's a minimum age. In general, per day, inexpensive is roughly $75–120, moderate $100–$175, and expensive $150 and up.

Hotels and Inns

The White Elephant
Easton Street
(508) 228–2500 (for reservations) or (800) ISLANDS
Seasonal. EP. C. Expensive.

The White Elephant is a lovely, sprawling hotel complex running along the north side of Nantucket Harbor between the Steamboat Wharf and Brant Point. Not only one of the Island's oldest, it is also one of its most charming hotels. There is a main building with regular hotel rooms and lovely dining facilities (the Brant Point Grill, 228–2500) overlooking the harbor. One room is available for the handicapped. Another building in the complex is The Breakers, which is the most expensive and elegant. It consists of lovely sitting/bedrooms, some with views of the harbor, and suites with private patios. Guests in The Breakers are greeted with wine and fresh flowers in their rooms. Complimentary continental breakfast and afternoon wine and cheese are included in the room fee at The Breakers. A concierge is on duty twenty-four hours a day to assist guests with everything from renting a sailboat to making a dinner reservation.

The White Elephant has its own docking facilities for small boats and a swimming pool. It is a very easy place to manage children; during July and August children ages five to twelve can enroll in their "For Kids Only" summer recreation program. The hotel is a short walk to the center of town.

White Elephant Cottages
Easton Street
(508) 228–2500
Expensive.

Part of this perfectly charming hotel complex are cottages that vary in size and price; eight with harbor view are adja-

BROWN AND WHITING

The White Elephant Resort.

cent to the main hotel grounds, and the others are nearby. They have one to three bedrooms, some have fully equipped kitchens, and all are attractively furnished. Occupants have full access to all the hotel facilities and services.

Where to Stay

53

Jared Coffin House
Built in 1845 by one
of the Island's most
successful shipown-
ers, the Jared Coffin
House has been a
very popular inn
since 1847.

M.C. WALLO

Jared Coffin House
29 Broad Street
(508) 228–2400 (for reservations)
Open year-round. EP. Expensive.

In 1845, the Jared Coffin House was built so sturdily of English brick with a roof of Welsh slate that it was saved from the devastating fire in 1846. It was the first three-story house on Nantucket and was built by Jared Coffin as a futile attempt to keep his wife happy on the Island. It became an inn in 1847, and over the years several other buildings have been added to the hotel complex to increase the number of guest rooms. Most of the guest rooms have colonial-style reproduction furnishings, and there's a formal dining room. Its taproom, with heavy, old, dark beams and pine paneling, is a typical nineteenth-century tavern.

Harbor House
South Beach Street
(508) 228–1500 or (800) ISLANDS
Open year-round. EP. C. Expensive.

For more than a hundred years, this Island landmark has been the setting for entertaining cultural and educational events year-round. The hotel, which has 112 rooms in the main building and adjoining cottages, offers every desirable amenity for its guests: room service; color TV with cable, video, and AM/FM radio in each room; complete business traveler services with excellent facilities for meetings; preferred reservations at restaurants; baby-sitting services; and resident tennis pro. There's musical entertainment nightly in the summer in the Hearth Lounge and special programs most weekends in the winter. A light lunch is available around a flower-encircled swimming pool, and lunch and dinner are also served on the patio in good weather. Wheelchair accessible. Dinner reservations recommended.

The Woodbox
29 Fair Street
(508) 228–0587
Open June through December. MAP. Moderate.

Built in 1709, The Woodbox is Nantucket's oldest inn. It has the hand-hewn beams, huge fireplaces with ovens, and low ceilings that are so typical of eighteenth-century houses. The small rooms are beautifully furnished with period antiques. The restaurant serves breakfast and dinner to the public also. Reservations are required.

Harbor House
The Harbor House was built in an attractive courtyard-type complex at
the end of a typical Nantucket street. These particular houses are superb
reproductions, with brick sidewalks and gaslights.

Ships Inn
Fair Street
(508) 228–0040
Open May through October. Continental breakfast
included. Moderate.

Built in 1812 by Captain Obed Starbuck, this charming whaling captain's house is located in a quiet area that is nonetheless very close to the center of town. It is beautifully furnished with antiques. Many of the rooms are named for ships under Starbuck's command. The house was also the birthplace of Lucretia Coffin Mott, the first woman abolitionist and advocate of women's suffrage. The restaurant and full-service bar are open to the public. Reservations are recommended.

The Wauwinet
120 Wauwinet Road
(508) 228–0145; Fax (508) 228–6712
Very Expensive.

This large turn-of-the-century hotel is located at the head of Nantucket Harbor 6 miles from town. It overlooks the gentle harbor bay and is a very short walk through the dunes to the ocean.

The twenty-five rooms and cluster of charming individual cottages are all very attractive and very expensive, and the amenities are extraordinary. Your bedroom is made up fresh two times a day. Use of the inn's mountain bikes and tennis courts, jitney service to town from morning until night, movies for your bedroom TV, and daily cheese, port, and sherry tastings are included in the room fees, and for those who like water sports, sail boats, kayaks, and rowboats are available! You may order a picnic lunch from Toppers, their restaurant, and the inn's launch will drop you anywhere along the shore for a private beach picnic.

For the ultimate quiet getaway far from the town's mid-

Ships Inn
The stark and spare influence of the Quakers is very apparent in this foursquare building. The railing and sidelights by the front door are the only exterior departures from this austerity.

summer crowds, this is ideal. A minimum of four nights may be required during the busiest times. Open mid-May through late October.

Bed and Breakfasts

The Corner House
49 Centre Street
(508) 228-1530
Open year-round. Inexpensive to moderate.

It is the casual, relaxed warmth and ambiance that lend a special charm to this bed-and-breakfast spot a few blocks from town but in a quiet area. With the bedrooms' four-poster beds, quilts, and mixture of English and American antiques and a few contemporary, comfortable pieces throughout, the atmosphere is that of an authentic seaport house. Some rooms have refrigerators and/or TV. There is a plentiful home-made continental breakfast and delicious afternoon tea; sandwiches and pastries are served either out on the terrace or beside a cozy fire on chilly days.

The Pineapple Inn
10 Hussey Street
(508) 228-9992; Fax (508) 325-6051
Moderate to expensive.

This elegantly renovated and refurnished 1858 captain's house has some very special amenities that will delight guests and add to their comfort. White marble bathrooms with separate heating units for bedroom and bath, air conditioning, cable TV, a telephone with voice mail, and computer access are some of the very special creature comforts provided for guests. The inn's owner formerly had his own restaurant, and the delicious continental breakfast specialties are spectacular and attractively served in the historic dining room or out on the terrace. The inn radiates Nantucket at its most charming and gracious. There is a ground floor suite with wheelchair access. With all these extra comforts, it makes a fall or spring weekend particularly inviting.

The charming dining room of the Pineapple Inn.

Sherburne Inn
10 Gay Street
(508) 228–4425
Open year-round. Moderate.

In a quiet corner close to town, this delightful inn has eight charmingly decorated rooms and fireplaced parlors on both floors inviting sociability with other guests. Wine and cheese, fresh flowers, or a picnic basket will be provided upon request. A delicious homebaked continental breakfast can be taken out to the attractive garden on those delightful dew-freshened summer mornings. Air-conditioning.

Martin House Inn
61 Centre Street
(508) 228–0678
Open year-round. Moderate.

In the heart of the historic district, a few blocks from Main Street, the elegantly decorated rooms here are spacious and

An antique-filled bedroom in the Sherburne Inn.

Frederick G. S. Clow

inviting, with a blend of antique furniture from different periods. A large Hepplewhite dining room table, a porch with white wicker furniture, and a pretty yard are your options for enjoying the delicious homebaked Continental breakfast. Some rooms have shared baths.

Centerboard Guest House
8 Chester Street
(508) 228–9696
Open year-round. Expensive.

This delightful Victorian house has only six rooms, and each is decorated with exquisite and unusual taste. All the woodwork was stripped and subtly tinted to blend with the furnishings in each room—the effect is striking. There are flowers, layers of lace-trimmed linens, a European feather mattress, four-poster bed, icebox, telephone, and TV in each room. The rooms vary in size and accommodations. The studio includes a full kitchen and private entry. A delicious Continental breakfast is served, and no smoking is allowed on the premises.

Summer House—Fair Street
27 Fair Street
(508) 228–4258
Open May through October. Moderate.

This is another of those charming Nantucket Quaker houses in the historic district that has become a delightful antiques-furnished guest house. It is in a nice, quiet location, but at the same time it is very close to town. Some guest rooms have a fireplace or canopied beds, and you may have the complimentary breakfast in your room. The grey stone wall, rose arbor, and lovely, renowned Shakespearean herb garden where breakfast is served provide just the setting a visitor to Nantucket would hope to find.

The Quaker House
5 Chestnut Street
(508) 228–0400
Open May to October. Moderate.

Located in the historic district, near the center of town, this is a real find—reasonably priced and attractively furnished rooms of good size. The fine restaurant is very good and is known for its modest prices. The *Los Angeles Times* calls it ". . . a cheerful, pretty place . . . one of your best stops for moderate-cost dining."

Cliff Lodge Bed and Breakfast
9 Cliff Road
(508) 228–9480
Open year-round. Inexpensive to moderate.

Only a stone's throw from Main Street, this 1771 former whaling master's home is charming and informal with a graceful flair. The twelve light, airy rooms decorated with Laura Ashley wallpaper, white eyelet linens, and English country antiques all have private baths, TV, and phone. The view from the roof walk of the harbor and vast expanse of Nantucket Sound is breathtaking. A Continental breakfast is available.

The Nantucket waterfront.

Apartments and Cottages

The following apartment and cottage accommodations are in addition to the ones that are part of the hotels listed in the Hotels and Inns section. There are many more.

Wharf Cottages
Swain's Wharf and Old South Wharf
(508) 228–1500 or (800) ISLANDS
Seasonal. C. Moderate.

These cottages on the harborfront wharves are a welcome respite ashore for yachtsmen while their boats are tied up at a slip outside the door. The cottages are very close together and very popular, so it's best to make reservations weeks or months in advance. They are large enough for two to eight people and include kitchen and dining area. Many have private decks. Linens are provided. The cottages are suitable for families with older children. Three-night minimum.

Accommodations: Outlying Areas

The following includes several places within a mile or less of town. They have ample grounds and are particularly inviting for children.

COURTESY BRUCE HARRISON

Boaters and landlubbers alike enjoy staying at the grey-weathered cottages on Swain's Wharf and Old South Wharf.

The accommodations in the areas fringing the shoreline of the Island require transportation—a car, moped, or bicycle. Siasconset has several stores and two restaurants, but other necessities must be bought in Nantucket Town. There are also a grocery store, restaurant, and marina at Madaket.

Cliffside Beach Club
Jefferson Avenue
(508) 228–0618
Open May through October. EP. C. Expensive.

This is a private club, but with all facilities available to non-member guests. It is a wonderful spot with a fine restaurant, which is open to the public. The beach club is located less than a mile from town on a broad beach of Nantucket Sound where the water gently laps the shore, the sand is as fine as salt, and the sunsets are spectacular.

Guest rooms, some studio apartments, suites, and a three-bedroom apartment are available; all are expensive. There are a double bed and sofa bed in each room, handmade by Nantucket craftspeople, and the front rooms each have a tiny deck right on the beach. There is wheelchair access. The 1920s ambiance in the lounge is charming, with cathedral ceiling, lovely quilts hanging from rafters, white wicker, and flowers everywhere, all well suited to this grey, weathered building.

Westmoor Inn
Cliff Road
(508) 228–0877
Open April to December. Breakfast included. C.
Moderate to expensive.

This charming inn, only ¾ of a mile from the center of town, has a lot to recommend it. Surrounded by two acres of lawn, with wonderful views everywhere, the inn offers large, attractive rooms, all with private baths. There are two suites. The delicious Continental breakfast is included, hors d'oevres and wine are served every afternoon, and box lunches are readily available.

Beachside Resort
31 N. Beach Street
(508) 228–2241/800–322–4433
Open April through December. C. Moderate to expensive.

A moderate walk from town and close to Jetties Beach, Beachside Resort is a motel-type building with more stylish furnishings—lovely rooms decorated with Laura Ashley prints, brass and iron beds, and the modern conveniences of television, videocassette players, and air-conditioning.

It's a delightful place out of town, with no parking problem, a pool, tennis courts next door, and that wonderful Jetties Beach nearby. It's ideal for children, and those under age eight may share a room with their parents at no charge. The charge for those over age eight is $5.00 per night. There is wheelchair access.

The Dolphin Guest House
10 North Beach Street
(508) 228–4028
Open Year-round. C. Moderate to Expensive.

This is a real find: Midway between town and Jetties Beach, 1½ blocks from the ferry, this twelve-room inn is a fine spot for children. It has TV, private baths, phones, and a common kitchen where you can pack a picnic or cook a little bite of food. The yard is delightful, and there are indoor and outdoor porches.

The Summer House
Siasconset
(508) 257–4577
Open May through October. EP. C. Expensive.

The Summer House is located in an attractive setting on a bluff at the edge of the sea. It consists of a main building and tiny, charming, grey-shingled cottages. An oddity for Nantucket, but something some visitors will enjoy, is a swimming pool right on the beach below the bluff. Lunch or cocktails may be enjoyed on the sand here. Lunch and dinner are

Where to Stay

served six days a week, and there's also a fine Sunday brunch in the restaurant (257–9976).

Wade Cottages
Siasconset
(508) 257–6308/(212) 989–6423
Open May through mid-October. C. Moderate.

Formerly a private estate, with some structures from the 1800s incorporated into those built in the late 1920s, Wade Cottages consists of rooms with private or semiprivate baths, apartments with one to four bedrooms, and cottages with three to five bedrooms. The large living room in the main building overlooking the ocean has the relaxing informality and character of a 1920s lodge—it's delightful. There is wheelchair access. It's a wonderful compound of old, shingled buildings. The grounds are spacious and attractive, with a sea view and private beach. Tennis, golf, and restaurants are nearby.

Youth Hostel
Surfside
(508) 228–0433
Open April through October. EP. Inexpensive.

This is, of course, a very popular spot for cyclists and backpackers. It is located in the old lifesaving station on the beach. The fee is $14 per night for members and $17 for nonmembers. There are forty-nine beds, cooking facilities, and it is open from April to October. The maximum stay is for three nights.

Dionis Cottages
Dionis Beach
(508) 228–4524
Open year-round. C. Moderate.

Just 2 miles from town, these five large cottages, one with four bedrooms, have central heat, fireplaces, complete kitchen facilities, and linens. They are right on the beach of the North Shore, where the swimming is gentler than in the ocean.

Nantucket Inn
27 Macy's Lane
(508) 228–6900 or (800) 321–8484
Open year-round. EP. C. Inexpensive to moderate.

This 100-room hotel and conference center at the airport is a complete departure from the familiar Island hostelry. It is a self-contained hotel with wheelchair access, indoor and outdoor pools, a health fitness center, tennis courts, banquet facilities, and a dining room. The furnishings are modern, there's ample parking, and free transportation is offered to town and the beach. Fine for children.

6

WHERE TO EAT

Nantucket is famous for its very fine food, and the number of restaurants has increased in the last few years until there are now about sixty-five, varying in size, price, and specialties. The following is a small sampling of the many choices available in various price ranges. The area code to use with phone numbers on Nantucket is (508).

Many restaurants request guests to come properly attired for dinner and this varies a bit. A couple require the men to wear jackets, the women to wear dresses or dressy slacks, others request guests to wear appropriate casual dress for dinner, and others are most informal, but none allow bathing suits. With the amount of time and effort Nantucketers dedicate to producing extraordinary, prize-winning gourmet meals, and out of courtesy to them, please note their suggestions. Some restaurants that are wheelchair accessible don't necessarily have special restrooms. It is best to inquire about this and also about payment; some places won't take any credit cards or personal checks, and others take only certain credit cards. For dinner, the average expensive restaurant is $25 per entree (a couple of them are very expensive with a minimum entree charge of $35 or more), the moderate ones are $15 to $25, and the inexpensive are up to $15 for a pizza, salad, or sandwich. A complete dinner in these wonderful upscale restaurants averaging $25 per entree is about $50 per person.

Expensive

Chanticleer
Siasconset
257–6231

Not only is this considered the Island's premier restaurant, but it is also rated as one of the best in the country. A car, taxi,

*The entrance to the flower-circled outdoor courtyard of the
exquisitely charming Chanticleer restaurant, where meals are
served outside depending on the weather.*

or the Island bus is necessary to get to this charming, rose-
covered cottage. It has been an island institution for years,
and Chef Jean-Charles Berruet is famous for his classic
French cuisine, which includes trout, saddle of rabbit, pheasant, Nantucket oysters, and other delicious entrees. The inn

has been the recipient of the *Wine Spectator*'s "Grand Award" many times. Reservations are required, and jackets are a must for men and casual but elegant dress for women. Very special and very expensive, the Chanticleer is open every day except Wednesday for lunch and dinner from late May to mid-October. There is access for the handicapped. Liquor served.

Le Languedoc
24 Broad Street
228–2552

Located in town, this delightful French restaurant has an upstairs dining room, attractive garden terrace, and cellar room. The handsome blue tiles around the fireplace, blue-checked tablecloths, candlelight, and flowers are the perfect complement to the fine, innovative American cuisine. There is a cafe menu available in the cellar room and on the terrace, and private dining rooms for eight to twelve people are available. Reservations for dinner are recommended, and wheelchair access is available on the terrace. Proper dress requested. The restaurant is open April to December for lunch and dinner. Liquor served.

Straight Wharf Restaurant
Straight Wharf
228–4499

Northern Italian and French cuisine are served here, including innovative vegetable choices and a Mediterranean diet with grains. The restaurant serves dinner only, daily except Mondays. It has a nice bar that opens in the late afternoon and offers a limited menu. No reservations are needed in the bar, and you can expect fast service here. Wheelchair accessible. Seasonal. Very expensive. Proper dress preferred.

The Club Car
1 Main Street
228–1101

The Club Car itself is from the old Nantucket Railway Company, which ran from town out to 'Sconset. It makes an attractive setting for the casual lunches, including their famous Maryland crab cakes. The adjacent dining room serves delicious Continental cuisine dinners, and reservations are required. The bar in the club car is open until 1:00 A.M. Casual but proper dinner attire preferred. Wheelchair accessible. Open May to December.

DeMarco
9 India Street
228-1836

Twenty years ago this delightful restaurant opened and soon became known for its superb northern Italian cuisine, light and healthful. The extensive menu changes often to take advantage of the local produce. The pastas, breads, and desserts are made on the premises daily. This charming upscale restaurant recommends reservations and smart, casual attire. It has an extensive wine list and is open April through October. Wheelchair accessible.

Jared Coffin House
29 Broad Street
228-2400

The Jared Coffin House has two restaurants. Jared's is a more formal dining room open for breakfast and dinner year-round, and downstairs is the Tap Room, a very popular year-round tavern with a bar, rich brown paneling, and heavy beams; with a roaring fire on cold nights, it certainly is reminiscent of the nineteenth century. Chowder, hamburgers, and other traditional American fare is available here and on the attractive patio in warm weather. Reservations are recommended in the upstairs dining room and proper attire requested. Wheelchair access is available, and there is a children's menu.

Brant Point Grill at the White Elephant
Easton Street
228-2500

Right on the harbor, this is certainly one of the Island's most elegant dining spots. The delicious New England cuisine is served on the terrace or in the charming dining room with its Chinese Chippendale chairs and summery decor. Open May to October for breakfast, brunch, lunch, and dinner. Piano bar for evening entertainment. Wheelchair accessible. Liquor served. Dinner reservations and proper casual attire recommended.

The Woodbox
29 Fair Street
228-0587

A little out of the way, but well worth the walk, this 1709 inn, Nantucket's oldest, radiates the Island's history. It is small, intimate, and extremely popular. The restaurant is open from June to October for breakfast and dinner, Tuesday through Sunday. Dinner is served in two seatings, reservations preferred. Recipients of a *Wine Spectator* award, the Continental cuisine is delicious and varied. No credit cards are accepted. Casually elegant dress. Smoke free.

Topper's
At the Wauwinet
228-8768

Lunch, dinner, and Sunday brunch are served in the dining room and out on the terrace in this handsomely restored inn at the far end of Nantucket Harbor. The menu isn't large, but their New American cuisine features delicious regional specialties beautifully served, and it is very expensive. They are recipients of the *Wine Spectator*'s Grand Award. Reservations are required, and complimentary jitney service from town is available. The dining room is wheelchair accessible. It is open May to October. Jackets for men and casually elegant dress for women requested.

Moderate to Expensive

American Seasons
80 Centre Street
228-7111

Both the indoor dining room and the terrace provide an attractive, cozy setting for the superb regional cuisine that is unusually creative. They have also received the *Wine Spectator*'s Award of Excellence. Open for dinner April through December. Wheelchair accessible. Reservations requested. Casual but neat attire preferred.

21 Federal
21 Federal Street
228-2121

The ambiance in the handsome Eighteenth-century house is really charming, providing the ideal setting for entrees prepared in both the new and traditional American cuisine. It is delicious and being Nantucket's Ivy League restaurant, very busy and, unfortunately, very haughty. Reservations and casual but dressy attire recommended. Open April through December. Wheelchair accessible.

Kendricks at the Quaker House
Center Street at Chestnut
228-9156

Candlelight and music set the scene for this attractive spot near the center of town. They complement the chef's delicious dinners of fish, lamb, and veal, in addition to a vegetarian speciality and other original entrees. The bar menu is served until 11:00 P.M. Open for dinner daily, lunch Monday to Friday, brunch weekends, casual but proper attire requested. Wheelchair accessible. Reservations suggested.

The Galley on Cliffside Beach
Jefferson Avenue
228-9641

Seated under an awning with a breathtaking sunset view across Nantucket Sound, a piano bar, and candlelight, guests are treated to an ideal setting for a summer evening's repast. The local garden produce and bounty from the sea is prepared in an original manner with particular emphasis on unusual fish courses. Open June to October. Reservations suggested. Elegant, casual dress. Lunch and dinner served; open from 11:30 A.M. to 11:30 P.M.

Cioppino's
20 Broad Street
228-4622

An attractive patio, a bar, and three dining rooms complete this attractive restaurant in the heart of town. The delicious entrees include hazelnut-crusted Salmon, grilled lobster tails, and San Francisco cioppino among others. The recipient of the *Wine Spectator's* Award of Excellence for the last four years, this restaurant is open May through October. Reservations accepted. Casual but neat attire.

Christians
17 Old South Road
228-5818

This new spot out of town is simply charming. The attractive Cape Cod house is the ideal setting for the natural wood tables and chairs, fresh flowers everywhere, and bright multicolored china.

The choices of appetizers, salads, and entrees—"Hoof, fowl and fin"—are delicious and quite special. That isn't surprising because the experienced chef/owners have worked in New York and San Francisco. All items are also available for carry-out. Full liquor licence. Casual but proper attire. Open for breakfast, lunch, and dinner in season; dinner off-season.

The Boarding House
Federal Street
228-9622

The charming nineteenth-century atmosphere of The Boarding House makes this an attractive setting for their contemporary classic cuisine served at lunch and dinner. Dinner is served on the attractive patio in warm weather. The menu is always changing and offers island-fresh fish and vegetables. The restaurant is open year-round Monday through Saturday. Reservations are requested. The terrace and ground floor are wheelchair accessible. Liquor service. Casual dress.

The Hearth at Harbor House
South Beach Street
325-1364

Meals at The Hearth are served on the outdoor patio during good weather. The menu features good, traditional food, with local fish specialties. Complimentary champagne is served with Sunday brunch. In summer, there is nightly entertainment with dancing in the lounge. Reservations are requested. The restaurant has handicapped access and is open year-round. There is a children's menu and inexpensive early-bird dinners. A light lunch is available and is served around a swimming pool, which is across the driveway and through a winding garden path. Wheelchair accessible. Casual dress.

'Sconset Cafe
Post Office Square, Siasconset
257-4008

After a bike ride across the Island, a stop at this attractive little cafe is the perfect spot for a rest. The smoked turkey sandwich with cheese and cranberry is a great favorite, and the dinner menu includes delicious fish, lamb, and beef selections. Open Memorial Day through October. Casual but neat attire preferred. BYOB.

Cafe Bella Vita
Lower Orange Street, 2 Bayberry Court
228-8766

If fine Italian cuisine is your preference, this charming spot a short distance from town, with no parking problem, is your answer. Open year-round, it has a spritely, colorful decor and a garden patio. There are unusual appetizers, eight pasta dishes, and Scampi alla Griglia and Veal alla Milanese are two of the favorites. Full bar. Wheelchair accessible. Smoke free.

Family and Take-Out

Inexpensive to Moderate

Nantucket Tapas
15 South Beach Street
228-2033

This delightful, different little bistro is a few blocks from the center of town. The little cafe tables are suitable for a lunch of unusual appetizers from around the world. The assortment of tapas are served on a "tapas tree," a wrought iron stand designed to hold three tapas. There are also smoked turkey and other sandwiches, salads, and wine and beer. Open daily for lunch and dinner from 11:00 A.M. to 11:00 P.M. Take-out also available.

Arno's
Main Street
228-7001

An Island institution, open year-round from 8:00 A.M. to 9:30 P.M., Arno's serves traditional American cuisine and has take-out. Right at the top of the square, it has a children's menu and handicapped access. Beer and wine served. Casual dress.

Fog Island Cafe
7 South Water Street
228-1818

A charming little spot a few steps from the harbor for early risers (7:00 A.M.), the cafe's salads, sandwiches, and breakfasts are very good. The service is excellent, dinners are delightful, and take-out is available. Open year-round. BYOB. Children's menu, casual dress, and smoke free.

Blackeyed Susan's
India Street
325-0308

Another delightful little cafe off Centre Street. Susan's menu for 7:00 A.M. breakfast includes traditional and unusual selections, and dinner offers traditional recipes with an ethnic twist. BYOB. It is delicious and a very popular spot, so reservations are recommended. Casual dress.

Moona
122 Pleasant Street
325-4301

This is exceptionally innovative gourmet food at moderate prices. The owners, Everett Reid and Joan Dion, were featured in the PBS series "Great Chefs of the East" and were also invited to do their second dinner at the prestigious James Beard House. It is located out of town where the parking is easy. Take-out available. Open Tuesday through Saturday at 5:30 P.M. for dinner. Casual but neat attire. Full liquor license. Wheelchair accessible. Reservations requested.

Espresso Cafe
Main Street
Year Round
228-6930

In the heart of town, this delightful European-style cafe

with its large garden patio in the rear is a lifesaver for weary visitors. The soups, salads, sandwiches, pizzas, croissants, and other fare are delicious. Open for breakfast, lunch, and dinner. Take-out. Casual dress.

Sea Grille
45 Sparks Avenue
325-5700

Out Orange Street at the rotary is a fine year-round restaurant open for dinner at 5:30 P.M. daily. It features nicely grilled chicken breast, lamb, ribs, and some fish selections. There's no parking problem. Wheelchair accessible. Liquor service. Recipients of a *Wine Spectator* Award of Excellence. Casual dress. Childrens menu, Smoke-free dining room.

Faregrounds Restaurant
27 Fairgrounds Road
228-4095

Just beyond the rotary on the road to Surfside, this attractive eatery is ideal for several reasons: reasonably priced, good, traditional American food; easy parking; space for children to run around waiting for dinner; a good children's menu, and take-out, including full menu. Open year-round. Liquor service. Wheelchair accessible. Smoke-free dining room, patio service, and casual dress.

Claudette's Catering
On the Square in Siasconset
257-6622

Claudette's is open May to October for catering parties, weddings, and dinners. It is also open seven days a week during the summer to provide box lunches, canopies and party foods, and clambakes to go. Liquor may be brought by patrons.

Food for Here and There
Lower Orange Street
228-4291

Delicious subs, pizzas, quiche, and fresh salads are readily available for here or to go. You may phone your orders ahead. They are open year-round from 10:00 A.M. to 10:00 P.M. daily, and there is ample off-street parking. Wheelchair access is available, and there is a children's menu.

Something Natural
50 Cliff Road
228-0504

The huge, tasty, double-size sandwiches here will appeal particularly to those with big appetites. The store also has natural foods, delicious salads, homemade breads and cakes, soft drinks, coffee, and tea. It is conveniently located in a lovely residential area; tables under the old trees are available. It is open April to October for breakfast, lunch, and dinner. Children's menu. BYOB. Casual dress.

The Downyflake
Harbor View Way
228-4533

Nantucketers are very partial to this tiny eatery/bakery located right on Children's Beach. It is renowned for its doughnuts and moderately priced traditional food. It is open for breakfast and lunch, as well as for take-out food, from April through mid-October. Downyflake also has a restaurant on Sparks Avenue that is open year-round. Casual dress.

Henry's
Steamboat Wharf
228-0123

If you want to pick up a delicious sandwich or grander fare while waiting for the ferry or heading to the beach, Henry's

M.C. WALLO

Brotherhood of Thieves
*This restaurant, known for its character and good food, is one of
the most popular places on Nantucket.*

has it. It is very good, not too expensive, and has been a
favorite with Nantucketers for years. This eatery is open on a
seasonal basis and has handicapped access.

Henry's Jr., 29 Orange Street, has the same delicious
grinders and sandwiches. The cheese specials are always a
favorite. It is open year-round.

Brotherhood of Thieves
23 Broad Street
(no listed phone)

Famous for its chowder and hamburgers, the Brotherhood has, according to several Island natives, the best atmosphere of any Nantucket restaurant; it is, therefore, one of the most popular places on the Island and very inexpensive. The name of the bar, "Brotherhood of Thieves," is taken from a pamphlet written by Stephen S. Foster on Nantucket in 1843 and titled "The Brotherhood of Thieves: Or a True Picture of the American Church and Clergy." It is open year-round (except in February) seven days a week for lunch and dinner. No credit cards are accepted. Wheelchair access is provided, and there is a children's menu. Liquor service. Casual dress.

Cap'n Tobey's Chowder House
Straight Wharf
228–0836 Seasonal

Down on the waterfront is this old Island favorite, with its tavern atmosphere and delicious, moderately priced food. As the name implies, the chowder and seafood are specialties; steaks, turkey, veal, and pork are also available, as well as a salad bar. Open daily from May to October for lunch and dinner, there is also liquor served. There is a children's menu and outdoor deck with a view of the harbor. Casual dress.

7

TELEPHONE NUMBERS & ADDRESSES

For your basic needs during your stay on the Island, here are some telephone numbers and addresses you will want to keep on hand.

General

For emergency only—fire, police or ambulance, call 911
Congdon's Pharmacy, 47 Main Street, 228–0020
Nantucket Pharmacy, 45 Main Street, 228–0180
Island Pharmacy, Sparks Avenue, 228–6400
Nantucket Cottage Hospital, South Prospect and Vesper Lane, 228–1200
Police Department, East Chestnut Street, 228–1212
Fire Department, Pleasant Street, 228–2323
Siasconset Fire Department, 228–2323
M.S.P.C.A. (Animal Hospital), Crooked Lane, 228–1491
U.S. Post Office, Federal Street, 228–1067
U.S. Post Office, Siasconset, 257–4402

Houses of Worship

Christian Science Society, Madaket Road, 228–0452
Congregation Shirat HaYam, Western Avenue, 228–6588
First Congregational, 62 Centre Street, 228–0950
First Baptist, 1 Summer Street, 228–4930
Interdenominational Nantucket Worship Center, High School, 228–5616
Jehovah's Witnesses, Milk Street, 228–8816
St. Mary's Roman Catholic, Orange Street, 228–0100
St. Paul's Episcopal, 20 Fair Street, 228–0916
Society of Friends (Quaker), 7 Fair Street

Union Chapel, Siasconset (summer season only) 257–6616
Unitarian, Orange Street, 228–5460
United Methodist, Centre Street, 228–1882

United Methodist Church
The Methodist Church was built on Centre Street in 1823. The striking Doric-columned front was added in 1840.

M.C. WALLO

Information, General

The Nantucket Visitors Service and Information Bureau offices are among the busiest spots on the Island during the summer. People working here can answer all your questions about the Island. The main office is at 25 Federal Street, off Broad Street, and the telephone number is 228–0925. Other seasonal offices are: Steamboat Wharf, 228–0929; Straight Wharf, 228–1929; and Airport, 228–2115.

The Nantucket Chamber of Commerce, now located at 48 Main Street in the middle of town square. Pacific Club Building at the foot of Main Street, also has helpful answers to general information questions about the Island. It has a publication filled with information. The telephone number is 228–1700.

Information, Historical

The office of the Nantucket Historical Association is located on Union Street off Main Street. The Association has preserved and continues to maintain fourteen old buildings and exhibits for the visitor. It prints a map and a brochure with information about each building and exhibit. There is one

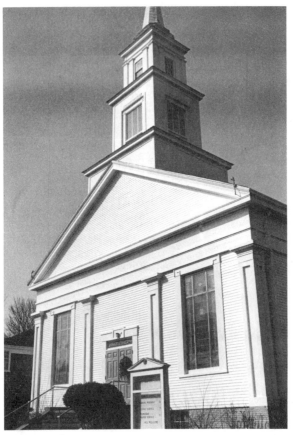

First Baptist Church
This handsome building on Summer Street was built in 1840, at a time when the Quaker religion was in a decline.

admission fee for all the exhibits or separate fees per exhibit.

The people in the office are most helpful to anyone seeking information about the Island's history. The Association's mailing address is Nantucket Historical Association, P.O. Box 1016, Nantucket, MA 02554. The telephone is 228–1894.

Library

The Nantucket Library is housed in the Atheneum at the corner of Federal and Lower India streets. The telephone number is 228–0666. The Maria Mitchell Association maintains a scientific library on Vestal Street (228–1110).

Newspapers

The *Inquirer and Mirror,* a weekly, is the Island's main newspaper. The magazine *Nantucket Magazine* is published four times a year. The two giveaway newspapers are *Yesterday's Island* and *Nantucket Map and Legend.*

The Hub, on Main Street at the corner of Federal Street, is the most popular newspaper store on the Island. Besides the local papers, it also has the *New York Times,* the *Boston Globe,* and many other urban papers.

Public Rest Rooms

When you are wandering through the town of Nantucket, you may want a rest room. Facilities can be found at the Information Bureau on Federal Street, on the waterfront at Children's Beach, and on Straight Wharf. There are also public rest rooms at some of the public beaches on the Island.

Public Telephones

You will find pay telephones at the Information Bureau, on the wharves, and on several main streets in town.

Zip Codes

The postal zip codes of Nantucket are 02554 and 02584. The code for Siasconset is 02564.

8

LEISURE ACTIVITIES

Nantucket summers burst with a great variety of sports, entertainment, and educational activities: sailing, fishing, swimming, golf, minigolf, tennis, racquet sports, bike races, running races, volleyball, art, music, theater, photography, basket weaving, pottery making, nature walks, bird-watching, windsurfing, marine science and wildlife instruction, and many lectures and musical programs of all descriptions. There are many attractive gift shops, some featuring unusual items made on the Island.

Antiques Galleries

Four things visitors to Nantucket hope to find—and they won't be disappointed—are exceptionally fine food, wonderful accommodations, beautiful beaches, and fine antiques. There are about two dozen antiques shops in town. Many of them specialize in certain things such as scrimshaw, nineteenth-century maritime paintings, artifacts, and furniture. Other shops sell Nantucket lightship baskets, which have become a unique Island logo, China Trade porcelains, old hooked rugs, country furniture, weather vanes, silver, and English antiques.

Art Galleries

Nantucket is a haven for artists who have found the light and scenery superb. There are more than forty galleries, and they carry everything from inexpensive prints to expensive oils. The first gallery, The Artists Association, which opened in 1945, is located on Washington Street and is active year-round. A recent book by John Villani, *The 100 Best Small Art Towns in America* (John Muir Publications, 1998), ranked Nantucket number 12.

Art Instruction

There are two places open year-round—as well as other places that are open only in the summer—where one may take art lessons. The length of the courses and the subject matter vary from year to year. The Nantucket Island School of Design and the Arts on Wauwinet Road has a huge summer program offering lectures, seminars, and college credit courses in drawing, painting, sculpture, printmaking, photography, and others. For more information, call 228–9248.

The Artists Association on Washington Street is open all year, offering courses in weaving, painting, pottery, and other disciplines. Their summer programs offer a wealth of courses in the arts for both adults and children. More information is available at 228–0294. There are others, so check with the Nantucket Information Bureau.

Astronomy

The Loines Observatory of the Maria Mitchell Association is open to the general public on clear Wednesday evenings during the summer. The association also conducts children's classes in astronomy. Seminars are presented by visiting scientists from various universities. There is also a lecture series of about twenty talks during the summer, again with many distinguished speakers. About half of these programs are slanted toward young audiences. The observatory is on Milk Street Extension, and its telephone is 228–8690.

Auctions

There are many auctions from spring through fall; some are for charity, and others are strictly commercial. A wide variety of items are offered. Check the newspapers for announcements.

Artists' Association of Nantucket Wet Paint Auction.

Beaches

Before you plan to take a four-wheel drive vehicle on the beaches, be sure to have proper permits and check the latest regulations. Smith's Point may be closed in June for Piping Plovers, and other areas may be closed or have some restrictions.

Nantucket beach sand is just right for stretching out or building sand castles, or walking on, for it's neither too fine nor too granular and pebbly. There are beaches on the harbor or Nantucket Sound side of the Island where the waves are very gentle. The beaches on the ocean have waves that average about 3 to 4 feet and sometimes build up to 6 feet or more after a storm.

There are three public beaches in town and five public beaches out of town. In town, Children's Beach on Harbor View Way, next to Steamship Wharf, has a lifeguard on duty and food, rest room facilities, a grassy area for play, and a playground. At Brant Point by the lighthouse at the harbor's entrance, there are no facilities, and the currents are strong, but it's a lovely spot to watch all the harbor activity and sunsets. Francis Street Beach, a small-harbor beach, is at the end of Washington Street. No lifeguard!

Near town is Jetties Beach on North Beach Street, along the north shore of the Island, west of Brant Point. This Nantucket Sound beach has lifeguards, rest rooms, bathhouses, a restaurant, tennis courts, and towels and chairs for rent.

Dionis Beach is 3 miles out of town on Nantucket Sound. It is located west of Jetties Beach, along the west shore; a broad, expansive beach with rolling sand dunes, it has a gentle surf, lifeguards on duty, and rest rooms.

Madaket Beach, approximately 5 miles from town, has ocean surf swimming. The currents are very dangerous around Smith Point. A lifeguard is on duty, and rest rooms and mobile food service are available.

Cisco Beach, in the Hummock Pond Road area, is a popular area on the Island for surfing. There is a lifeguard but no other facilities. The beach is approximately 4 miles from the center of town.

Surfside Beach on the south shore is one of the most popular swimming spots on the Island. There is surf swimming here under the watchful eyes of the lifeguards. Located

Surfside Beach, arguably the Island's most popular beach.

FREDERICK G. S. CLOW

Leisure Activities

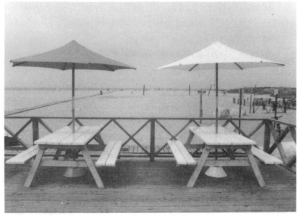

Jetties Beach, located on the west side of the Island, has tennis courts, a restaurant, lifeguards, and bathhouses.

approximately 3 miles from town, the beach is reached by direct bus service as well as by bicycle path. A bathhouse, small snack bar, rest rooms, public phones, lifeguards, and the ever-present bicycle stand make this a convenient place to spend a day.

Codfish Park, the town beach at Siasconset, is approximately 7¹/2 miles from town. Bus service is provided from town, and there is also a bicycle path. It is surf swimming here, and sometimes there is seaweed. A lifeguard is on duty, and playground equipment is provided.

Tom Nevers, next to 'Sconset, has a pebbly beach, heavy surf, and no lifeguard.

Berry Picking

If has reached the point where there are so few berry bushes left on the Island that the visitor is advised not to pick any berries. The same is true for wild grapes. The much-touted beach plum is not quite as prevalent on Nantucket as it is on the Cape, and the huge cranberry bog at Gibbs Pond is a private business. Several products, however, including native jams and jellies, cranberry jelly and chutney, as well as honey from the hives alongside the bog, are available in Nantucket's shops. The Museum Shop, next to the Whaling Museum, is an excellent spot for such goods.

Bird-watching

Nantucket is a joy for the bird-watcher. The birds are everywhere in the summer; songbirds live inshore, while ducks, geese, terns, egrets, and others haunt the marshes and ponds to nest and feed. Nantucket is right on the migratory path of many birds, so in the winter months Arctic seabirds take refuge in Island waters. During the summer, the Maria Mitchell Association's Natural Science Department sponsors bird walks three mornings a week, and they have become increasingly popular. For further details call the Hinchman House at 228–9198.

Boat Rentals and Instructions

Nantucket waters are wonderful for sailing, motorboating, and fishing. There are small outboards, sailboards, and sailboats available for rent. Sport-fishing boats are available for charter either by the day or half day. The larger yachts offer dinner cruises or may be chartered by private parties. Check with the newspaper or Nantucket Information Bureau to see what's available.

Children's Activities

Children's Beach, with slides, swings, the Downyflake sandwich bar, and gentle surf, is wonderful for youngsters, but when they have had too much sun, there are several other activities provided just for them. The Nantucket Library, in the Atheneum on Lower India Street, offers a story hour on Saturday mornings. Call 228–1110 for more details.

The observatory of the Maria Mitchell Association offers astronomy lectures on Tuesday mornings. Its telephone number is 228–9273. The Association's Natural Science Museum at the Hinchman House holds nature classes for children. Call 228–9198.

The Chamber Music Center at the Coffin School (228–2505) provides music lessons; the Artists Association on Straight Wharf (228–0722) gives art lessons; and sailing lessons are available from a number of boat rental companies.

The Nantucket Island School of Design and the Arts (228–9248), located in an old, converted cow barn on Wauwinet Road, offers an extraordinary number of courses in the arts for adults and children. Their summer programs for children, ages four to fifteen, include painting, drawing, collage, clay, and performance.

Miniature golf, which seems to be having a revival in the country, is located at Nobadeer and Sun Island roads, near the airport, and is delightful fun for all ages. There are Children's Theatre amateur productions. A Pirate and Mermaid Parade is part of the Harborfest activities at the end of June.

The Nantucket Community Day Camps offer baseball, softball, basketball, soccer, field hockey, and lacrosse instruction for children. The Sandcastle Contest at Jetties Beach in mid-August has become extremely popular for children as well as adults.

Concerts

The Musical Arts Society's professional musicians give concerts on six Tuesday evenings during July and August at the First Congregational Church. Call 228–0950 for more information.

The Arts Council gives Friday evening performances at the Methodist Church from September to June but does not perform in the summer.

The Nantucket Chamber Music Center has two choral and instrumental concerts a year, one in the spring and one in the fall. Call the Coffin School (228–2505) for more details.

Band concerts are held every Sunday at 7:00 P.M. during July and August in the gazebo at Harbor Square down on the waterfront.

Noonday concerts with guest soloists and ensembles are held every Thursday in July and August at the Unitarian Church at 11 Orange Street.

There are also many nationally known popular singers and bands to be heard throughout the summer, including performances of folk music, sea chanteys, rock, reggae, and other programs.

Evening Entertainment

The following places have a piano player or other musicians performing in their bars until closing: The Brotherhood of Thieves, Chanticleer, the Tavern, the White Elephant, the Club Car, the Nantucket Inn, the Whale Restaurant, and the Rose and Crown Restaurant. There is dancing nightly at the Harbor House, The Chicken Box on Dave Street, and The Muse on Atlantic Avenue.

Check with the various boat rental places if you're interested in an evening sunset sail. The availability of boats changes from season to season.

There are restaurants that prepare clambakes, which can be taken to the beach for an evening picnic. The sunset over Nantucket Sound makes these beaches beautiful in the early evening.

There are lectures, movies, concerts, art gallery shows, and plays on different evenings. All the inns and hotels have a calendar of events.

Fall Foliage

According to a recent study, there are now 1,270 plant species on the Island. Wildflowers should *never* be picked; but you may gather dried grasses in the fall for arrangements, and this will not do harm to the plants. The salt hay and other marsh grasses, brown milkweed pods, bayberry, and bittersweet make attractive fall bouquets. The cattail found in brackish water around the edges of marshes is the less common, narrow-leafed variety. It has crossbred, as often happens on the Island, and slim, medium, and fat ones can be

Lush foliage surrounds this freshwater inland creek.

found. There is still plenty of wild grape on the Island, and the vines can be cut to make wreaths, assuming one has permission from the property owner.

Fishing

Fish abound in the shoal waters swirling around the Island, as well as in the calmer harbor and lagoons.

Bluefish, flounder, scup, bonita, codfish, striped bass and black sea bass are the most familiar. For the sport fisherman, bluefish, marlin, sailfish, and bonita are the true game fish and the most desirable. Bluefish not only put up a good fight, but also are very plentiful alongshore from May through October. Charter boats are available by the day or half-day to go out in the rips to fish, or one can surf cast for the fish along the Island's south and east shores.

In midsummer, swordfish prefer the warm waters of the Gulf Stream, which is about 60 to 80 miles southeast of Nantucket. They are very scarce now but can be caught—if you are lucky—with a harpoon. They are also caught commercially by long lining (which is just that, a very long line with hooks on it). Years ago, swordfish were caught within 10 miles of the Island, but like all species that become very popular, they have become scarce.

The Atlantic bonita is another popular game fish with the sportsman. Large schools of them usually arrive in Nantucket Sound around the first of August and are gone by October. Years ago large catches were made in gill nets all through the month of September.

Overfishing and pollution made the once-popular striped bass very scarce along the East Coast. Striped bass fishing was banned for several years. The moratorium was successful, and striper fishing is now permitted.

The bottom fish—flounder and scup—are found in quiet water, such as Nantucket Harbor, as well as the shoals offshore. They can be caught from a rowboat, or a favorite method for young children is to drop a hook and line off a dock, using quahog meat for bait. These fish are good to eat, although flounder have become scarce.

The codfish is a winter fish that by June has gone offshore to deeper water. It is as delicious and prevalent in Nantucket waters as the eel but is far more popular. At the turn of the century and later, eels were often caught through the ice and shipped to New York City, particularly at Christmastime; the Italians there considered them a delicacy. Both cod and eel were also salted and exported.

The Island bookstores have various titles that describe all the fish that are found in waters around the Island.

Flight Instruction

Flight instruction is available at the Nantucket Memorial Airport, which is located on the south side of the Island, 3 miles from town. For more information, call 325-5300.

Golf

There are two public, nine-hole golf courses on the Island: the Siasconset Golf Club (257–6596) and the Miacomet Golf Club on Hummock Pond Road (325–0334). Both are open all year. The eighteen-hole Sankaty Head Golf Club is private, but it is open to the public after October 15 (257–6391). The new Nantucket Golf Club off Milestone Road in 'Sconset is also private. There is also miniature golf near the airport. The courses are never crowded on those off-season days when the weather is pleasant.

Kite Flying

Many shops sell colorful kites, and the beaches lend themselves beautifully to this popular pastime.

Lectures

The Maria Mitchell Association (228–0898 or 228–9198) has lectures on astronomy, nature, botany, and birds that are held throughout the year. The Atheneum's series of book and author lectures are among the most popular. Most are free and people get the opportunity to meet authors of some current best sellers. There are many, many other lectures, too, so check with the Nantucket Information Bureau.

Museums

Whaling Museum, Broad Street
Fair Street Museum, 7 Fair Street
Thomas Macy Warehouse, Straight Wharf (second floor)
Life Saving Museum, Polpis Road
Maria Mitchell Association Museums (open mid-June through August):
    Aquarium, 29 Washington Street

Birthplace, 1 Vestal Lane
Natural Science Museum, 7 Milk Street
Astronomical Observatory, 3 Vestal Street
Loines Observatory, Milk Street Extension
Library, 2 Vestal Street

Music Instruction

The Nantucket Chamber Music Center at the Coffin School on Winter Street has teachers to give lessons, year-round, in voice, piano, violin, and other stringed instruments. For further details, call 228–2505.

Nature and Wildflower Walks

The Maria Mitchell Association's Natural Science Department (228–9198) sponsors nature and bird walks as well as seminars and workshops for adults and children. They have a very interesting, varied schedule so it's best to inquire. The department also has a pamphlet for sale for a self-guided walk to Eel Point.

The Gulf Stream passes just 200 miles south of Nantucket on its way due northeast to Ireland; this accounts for the Island's extraordinary vegetation, which is a treasure trove to botanists. A meeting ground for northern and southern plants, unlike any other place in the country, the Island supports more than one thousand varieties of plant life. The prickly pear cactus one associates with the Midwest blooms in July on Coatue not far from the reindeer moss and wintergreen usually found in northern climates. Holly trees and hawthorns thrive in the mild climate. Plants brought over from Europe for their medicinal qualities now grow wild: Horehound, catnip, spearmint, peppermint, yarrow, bonsai, and tansy can be found. Scotch broom and heather blanket the moors, the deliciously fragrant wild azalea is found in the swamps, and the sweet smell of pink and white wild roses are found all along the roads and on the moors.

Shell Collecting

Brant Point, Pocomo, and Dionis beaches are the best places to find shells, though Nantucket doesn't have an exotic collection. The favorite is the lovely, fluted scallop shell, which has been used throughout history in designs on fine china and furniture and as a religious symbol.

Shellfishing

The location of clams, oysters, and mussels won't be included in this book because of the rapidly increasing number of people visiting Nantucket. This is a business for the native Islanders who, for the most part, earn their living on a seasonal basis. You may enjoy this wonderful New England seafood in many of the fine restaurants on the Island. Restaurants also serve lobster, which is so popular that demand sometimes outstrips supply and they have to be shipped in from Maine.

You may, after obtaining the proper permit, fish for the delicious bay scallop that is harvested only in the wintertime. It is the most valuable shellfish, other than the lobster. The season usually begins in November and goes until the end of March. There is a heavy fine for anyone harvesting scallops from spring through fall. Both in Nantucket Harbor and out in the shoal water off Tuckernuck Island, scallopers are out in force the first day of the season, dredging the bottom. There is a limit per day for each fisherman. The part you eat is the muscle, although the rest of the scallop is perfectly edible. Most of the scallops are shipped off the Island.

Shopping

Nantucket has become known for the quality of the merchandise in its gift and clothing stores. The handmade sweaters, materials, various crafts, and clothing at the Nantucket Looms on lower Main Street at the corner of Union Street are very popular. The many shops attractively display country furniture made from antique woods, china, glass, interesting weather vanes, and, beautiful needlepoint from Erica Wilson, who has a home on the Island. The work of local craftspeople in everything from candles to quilts is featured in many of the stores. The latest fashions by Lily, Hilfiger, Ralph Lauren and others are featured in various shops. The famous lightship basket has become an Island insignia, and its image is found on jewelry and china as well. There are also the usual number of souvenir shops, particularly along the waterfront.

When you're looking for a good book to read on the beach, you'll want to try Mitchell's Book Corner at 54 Main Street, an Island landmark, the newspaper store, the Bookworks at 25 Broad Street, and Logos on Washington Street.

Stables

Serenity Farm, Surfside, and Mt. Vernon Farm on Hummock Pond Road have fully equipped boarding facilities, complete with indoor riding areas and outdoor jump courses, schooling areas, and pasture. The stables are for people who have their own horse or who wish to lease one for the summer—there are no hourly or daily leases available.

Tennis

The pleasant weather of Nantucket makes it an enjoyable place to play tennis, and reservations are generally suggested. Try Nantucket Public Courts, Jetties Beach (May–October, 325–5334); Brant Point Racquet Club, North Beach Street (228–3700); Tristam's Landing, Madaket (228–4588); The Nantucket Inn (228–6900); or the Wauwinet Inn (228–0145), by reservation only.

Theaters

There are three theaters on the Island that show movies. The Dreamland Theatre on South Water Street (228–5356) shows movies through the summer season only. The

Siasconset Casino (257–6585), a private tennis club, shows current movies during summer evenings to the public. The Gaslight Theatre on North Union Street (228–4435) is open year-round.

For years Nantucket has had very active, sophisticated theater groups, visiting professional musicians, and a Dance Festival, including the Alvin Ailey Repertory Ensemble from New York.

The Theatre Workshop (Bennett Hall, 228–4305), next to the Congregational Church, presents plays using amateur actors who live on the Island as well as professionals. These plays are very popular, summer and winter. The Actor's Theatre has a summer program of live theater with a mix of professional and amateur actors, and Island Stage has programs all summer.

Walking Tours

The best way to become acquainted with the town is to take at least one (and preferably all) of the three tours of Nantucket that are described in this book.

There are also many other tours available: literary tours, birding tours, whale-watching and harbor tours, a natural history tour from Wauwinet to the Great Point Lighthouse and around Coatue to the harbor entrance, and a detailed tour of the historic spots in town.

Whale Watching

Nantucket Whalewatch takes visitors offshore for a day to the Great South Channel to see the whales, dolphins, and seabirds. These large whale-watching vessels have a galley for those who don't bring their own lunch. They leave from Straight Wharf several days a week, from mid-July to mid-September. These cruises have become very popular, and reservations can be made at (800) 322–0013, or you can inquire at the wharf when the vessels are in port. The cost for adults is $40, children under twelve, $22.

Wildlife Sanctuaries

Approximately one-third of the Island is now protected from development by several organizations. If you wish to explore wildlife sanctuaries, go to the Nantucket Conservation Foundation on Cliff Road (about a mile from town), where the staff will give you brochures and useful instructions concerning the sanctuaries. The three-hour Great Point Tour of the Coscata-Coatue Wildlife Refuge, sponsored by the Trustees of Reservations, is very popular. There are many other guided tours, nature walks, and bird-watching programs.

Winter Activities

NICOLE GRANT/INQUIRER AND MIRROR

Visitors frequently ask about what Nantucketers do in the winter. The activities are varied and most interesting, and many are available to the visitor. A large number take place at the Harbor House, while other programs are held at the library, churches, or the Coffin School. They include a series of concerts at the Harbor House; cribbage, backgammon, billiards, and bridge tournaments; theater groups; and the popular Dart League, which competes with teams on Cape Cod. There are soccer and softball teams, road races, ice skating, kayaking, swimming (indoor), excellent cooking classes, bike races, table tennis tournaments, lectures, literature discussion groups, lightship basket weaving, woodcarving

Ice-boating on a frozen pond during a brief Island cold spell.

Sledding at Deadhorse Valley is a great way to enjoy a Nantucket snowfall.

classes, art lessons, photography instruction, and programs at the Maria Mitchell Association. There are the Muse and The Chicken Box, a very popular spot where they have darts, billiards, musicians on stage, food, and liquor.

Yacht Racing

The Nantucket Yacht Club holds a series of races all summer for the various classes of small and large sailboats. The Opera House Cup Race in August for wooden boats includes many of the old 12-meter America Cup vessels. The mega-sailing-yachts, which are 60–140 feet in length,

Senator Edward M. Kennedy and Senator John F. Kerry at the Opera Cup race, 1997.

race in the Nantucket Bucket in August, and the Walter Gilman Page Memorial Sailing Regatta at Madaket in August includes three separate classes of boats. The Swan Regatta is in late July, and the Broward Annual Rendezvous of large yachts gathers for a late August weekend. There are also windsurfing races throughout the season. Inquire at the chamber of commerce for details.

U.S. Senator's race, 1998 Opera Cup, with Senator Frank R. Lautenberg at the helm of Easterner.

9

Tour I: The Center of Town

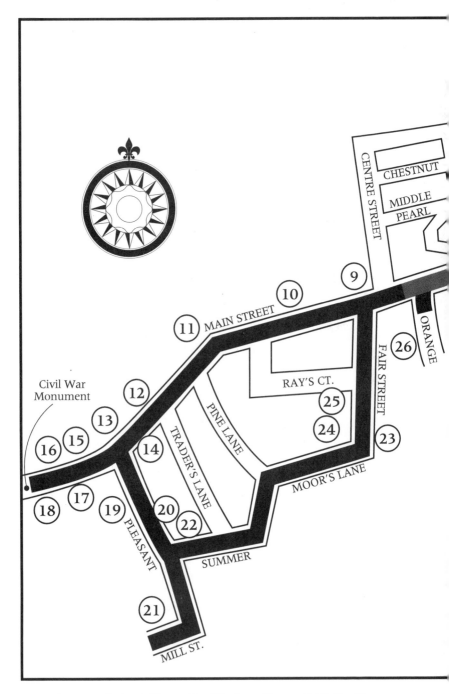

1. *Nantucket Harbor* 2. *Thomas Macy Warehouse Museum* 3. *Whaling Museum*
4. *Peter Folger Research Center* 5. *Main Street Square* 6. *Pacific Club*
7. *St. Mary's Roman Catholic Church* 8. *Nantucket Atheneum* 9. *Pacific Bank and Methodist Church* 10. *John Wendell Barrett House* 11. *Henry Coffin House and Charles Coffin Houses* 12. *Mathew Crosby House* 13. *The Three Bricks*

START ★

STEAMBOAT WHARF

3   1

OAK

EASY

SOUTH WATER

OLD NORTH WHARF
STRAIGHT WHARF

2

5   6

STREET
UARE

OLD SOUTH WHARF
COMMERCIAL WHARF

CANDLE

OLD WHALE

NEW WHALE

COMMERCIAL

TOUR I : THE CENTER OF TOWN
NANTUCKET

14. *William Hadwen Houses* 15. *Thomas Macy II House* 16. *Christopher Starbuck House* 17. *Zaccheus Macy House* 18. *Richard Gardner House* 19. *William Crosby House* 20. *Walter Folger House* 21. *Moor's End* 22. *Baptist Church* 23. *St. Paul's Episcopal Church* 24. *Quaker Meeting House* 25. *Fair Street Museum* 26. *Unitarian Church or Old South Tower*

This tour of Nantucket should be done on foot and is designed for those with limited time. You'll find that the twisting lanes and alleyways paved in brick and cobblestone have names that reflect global voyages. The houses themselves are usually named after the original owner, a practice that is followed in many New England towns where such things can be easily traced. The Nantucket Historical Association has preserved fourteen old buildings and exhibits for the visitor that are found on these first two tours. A visitor's pass to these buildings is $10.00 per adult and $4.00 for children ages five to fourteen. This pass can be obtained at any of these properties. Separate admissions to any one building are available at $3.00 or $4.00 per adult.

1. Nantucket Harbor

The Nantucketer, he alone resides and riots on the sea; he alone in Bible language, goes down to the sea in ships; to and fro plowing it as his own special plantation.
—Herman Melville, *Moby Dick*

Walking up from Steamboat Wharf you will come to Easy Street, on your left, which will take you over to the four other wharves on the harborfront. The first one you come to is Old North Wharf, which is privately owned. The next street you come to is Dock Street, and just beyond is the lower end of Main Street leading right out to Straight Wharf, which is full of gift shops and restaurants. The next two wharves, Old South and Commercial (also called Swain's), have shops, art galleries, and tiny rental cottages along the piers. Beyond them is the town pier for commercial fishing boats.

Early morning at Old North Wharf.

Walter Beinecke, Jr., bought and restored or rebuilt this whole area beginning in 1962, preserving the cobblestone mall lined with electrified reproductions of old gaslights and beautiful shade trees. The weathered, grey-shingled cottages out on the piers have the small-paned windows and white trim of all the old buildings; they are reproductions built by Beinecke to retain the special character of the town. Other buildings are original scallop shanties and boathouses. Wandering along these wharves, with their art galleries, gift shops, and restaurants, the visitor will also see sailboats and motorboats of every size and description tied to the piers.

It was, of course, Nantucket's large, protected harbor that created the town and the sea that molded her human history and provided her wealth. In the nineteenth century this whole waterfront area looked quite different; it was cluttered, messy, and smelly. In 1828 Daniel Webster was so surprised when he visited Nantucket he later reported in a speech in the U.S. Senate: "Nantucket itself is a very striking and pecu-

Nantucket Lightship
The famous Nantucket lightship, now a museum, pays a
visit to the island.

John Wendell Barrett House
One of the town's most elegant homes, this Greek Revival
house was built at 72 Main Street by John Wendell
Barrett, president of the Pacific Bank.

Pacific Club
The Pacific Club's building on Main Street Square was
originally shipowner William Rotch's countinghouse. The
iron drinking fountain for horses in the foreground is a
town landmark (right).

liar portion of the National interest. There is a population of eight or nine thousand persons, living here on the sea, adding largely every year to the National wealth by the boldest and most persevering industry."

Mary Cushing Edes in 1835 wrote to her sister, Charlotte Cushing, who lived outside of Boston: "The streets are sandy and they run in every direction. When you go out walking you return with shoes full of dirt, although some of the streets have sidewalks. The houses set any way. Travel over rutted roads is mostly in a calash, a two wheel open box wagon and standing mostly to soften the jolting. It is good fun once in a while but such exercise is not desirable often. You never saw anything like the place."

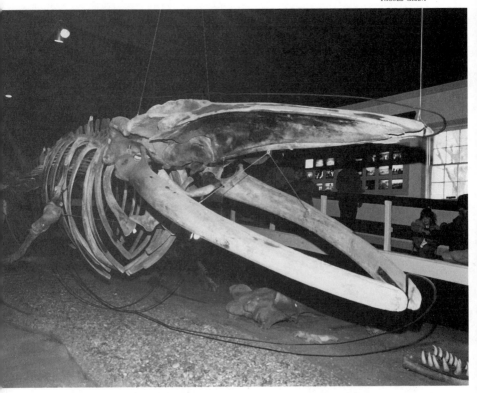

The Whaling Museum houses many eighteenth- and nineteenth-century whaling-industry artifacts.

In her book *Nantucket Landfall*, Dorothy Blanchard had a more romantic view of the waterfront and wrote of "the odor of whale oil and salt ocean pleasantly shot with the fragrances of Cadiz olives, Sicilian oranges, Smyrna figs, muscatel raisins, Oriental spices and teas." brought in from those protracted whaling voyages to the South Seas, the Indian Ocean, and China. With a population of 8,000 or more and a whaling fleet of over one hundred vessels, Nantucket was one of the busiest and wealthiest ports in America.

2. Thomas Macy Warehouse Museum
Straight Wharf

At the head of Straight Wharf, this Island landmark now has a gift shop on the first floor. Upstairs the Nantucket Historical Association has changing exhibits that may include a wonderful selection of nineteenth- and early twentieth-century photographs of summer vacationers on holiday.

Thomas Macy was a majority shareholder in whaleships. He was also a cooper, blacksmith, postmaster, and leading political figure.

3. Whaling Museum
Broad Street

Return on Easy Street to the head of the Steamboat Wharf and go left 1 block to the corner of South Beach and Broad Street, where you will find a museum on your right that is managed by the Nantucket Historical Association. The building of the Whaling Museum was originally a candle factory built in 1847. A guided tour by the museum staff explains how the various items on exhibit were used in whaling. There's a replica of the type of brick tryworks used on the deck of a whaleship to boil down the "liquid gold." Other whaling instruments, such as harpoons, lances, bailers, skimmers, and a whaleboat, scrimshaw, and ship models are also on display. And there's a jawbone of a whale that rises two stories, giving the visitor some idea of the extraordinary skill it must have taken to harpoon a whale. The admission charge is $4.00.

Also at the museum are the Nantucket lightship baskets. In the mid-nineteenth century lightships were stationed off the south and east ends of the Island to protect the transatlantic maritime traffic from the treacherous shoal waters swirling around Nantucket. The first South Shoal Lightship was stationed 24 miles out at sea in 1856 with a crew of ten men who were assigned several months of duty at a time. Another was the Cross Rip Lightship.

Just as the whaler turned to scrimshaw to while away the long dreary hours at sea, some of the men living aboard the lightships wove baskets that were used to carry everything from wood to vegetables. By 1905 the South Shoal Lightship was automated, and the men came ashore. The basket making continued, however, and these retired seamen sold them to summer tourists. The baskets developed in several stages through the years, from the loosely woven utilitarian Indian baskets, to heavy-duty farm baskets for carrying wood and produce, to the beautifully made handbags we know today that were the inspiration of José Reyes and the Sayle family.

José Reyes, a Filipino, came to the Island right after World War II to teach Spanish. Unable to find a job, he turned to basket making, and around 1947 he made a basket and, at her request, a mahogany top for Charlie Sayle's wife. A carver, writer, and veteran of the coastwise schooner trade, Charlie later carved a black ebony whale that his wife suggested they put on top of the basket. They showed it to José, who liked it so much that Charlie began carving the fittings and ivory decoration for the tops. The rest is history; the design has become the Island's principal insignia.

The basket pocketbooks immediately became popular, and today the tradition is carried on by Charlie Sayle's son and daughter-in-law, Bill and Judy Sayle, as well as others. There are many sizes and types of baskets for sale, and the design is also found on jewelry, china, and in all shapes and sizes.

The Museum Shop next to the museum is filled with attractive gifts, many of them unique to the Island.

4. Peter Folger Research Center
Broad Street

The first floor of the research center, which is right next to the Whaling Museum, houses a wonderful collection of paintings, furniture, and other historic artifacts that highlight the Island's history. The second floor is now a research center, open by appointment only, with a superb library that is invaluable to historians researching the Island's rich heritage.

5. Main Street Square

Leaving the Whaling Museum, go straight across the street onto South Water Street and continue until you come to the foot of Main Street.

The center of the town is a very broad, cobblestone square approximately 3 blocks long, with attractive shops in the old brick buildings lining either side of the street. The old drinking fountain for horses, in the middle of the street at the foot of the square, was moved from upper Main Street to its present location at the turn of the century.

The cobblestones were laid in 1837 to prevent the wheels of wagons, laden with heavy oil casks, from sinking into the sandy streets. They had been brought back as ballast in whaleships that returned from voyages with little cargo. Granite slabs, used in places as curbstones, were also brought back as ballast.

After the devastating fire in 1846, when hundreds of buildings were destroyed, it was decided to greatly broaden Main Street and to rebuild it with brick and slate to help avoid another such catastrophe. The lower part of the square was made rectangular, and marble slabs were set at the street corners as monuments. (Many of these have disappeared.) The brick sidewalks are wide, allowing room for benches, and the Bartlett Farms traditional vegetable-and-flower cart is always there. The two Pacific buildings face one another at either end of the square: The Pacific Club at the lower end and the

Main Street Nantucket USA, famous for its cobblestones and magnificent whaling captains' houses.

Pacific Bank at the upper. They not only add to the symmetry of this handsome center, but also act as constant reminders of the town's historic roots.

6. The Pacific Club
Main Street

The Pacific Club at the foot of the square was originally built in 1772 by William Rotch, the successful shipowner whose vessels *Beaver* and *Dartmouth* were involved in the famous Boston Tea Party. He was famous for his defense of the black sailor, Boston, and his ship *Bedford* was the first vessel to enter a British port after the Revolution. Rotch designed the building as a warehouse for oil and candles used in direct trade with London. The building also was used as a customhouse. Destroyed by the 1846 fire, it was rebuilt. In 1854 a group of former whaling shipmasters who had sailed the Pacific formed a club and they bought the building in 1861. Here they gathered to spin yarns of a lifetime at sea and play cribbage and whist. More than a century old, the club is still active and the rooms are now shared with a marine art gallery. The offices of the Nantucket Island Chamber of Commerce are on the second floor.

7. St. Mary's Roman Catholic Church
Federal Street

Walk up Main Street about 2 blocks and turn right on Federal Street. A short distance down on your right is St. Mary's Roman Catholic Church. Catholicism came late to Nantucket, and services first began in the Old Town Hall in 1849. In 1858, Harmony Hall on Federal Street was consecrated as St. Mary's Church. Then in 1896 the old building was removed and replaced by the present structure.

8. Nantucket Atheneum
Lower India Street

Farther along, at the corner of Federal and lower India Streets, is the Atheneum, a handsome Greek Revival building, which is the Nantucket Library. The original library was

Nantucket Atheneum

Nantucket's beautiful library holds a series of lectures throughout the summer. Most, but not all, of these interesting cultural events are free. Speakers in these summer series have included Tim Russert of "Meet the Press," historian Alfred Chandler, Jr., Stephen Ambrose (whose book *Undaunted Courage: Meriwether Lewis, Thomas Jefferson and the Opening of the West* has been made into a TV miniseries), David Hablestram, Russell Baker of the *New York Times*, and other notable writers.

Tim Russert and author/attorney Robert Mooney, left, at the Unitarian Church to benefit the Nantucket Atheneum.

completely destroyed in the terrible fire of 1846, when many valuable old books were lost. It was rebuilt within six months; no expense was spared, which was extraordinary considering the terrible plight of the town at the time. It was designed by Frederick Coleman, who, with his brother John, was an architect for many of the most beautiful buildings in town.

9. *Pacific Bank and the Methodist Church*
Main Street

Return to Main Street. Up at the head of the square, five streets come together (Fair, Orange, Centre, Liberty, and Main, with a few steps between). The Pacific National Bank, which faces the Pacific Club and also reminds the visitor of the importance of the Pacific Ocean in Nantucket's history, was built in 1818 of imported pressed brick. Its solid exterior is matched by its solvent interior, for it came through both the great fire of 1846 and the 1929 stock market crash unscathed!

Next to the bank is the United Methodist Church, which was built in 1823 just as Nantucket was forging into its golden era and the Quaker faith was beginning to wane. The Doric-columned front was added in 1840.

Across from the Main Street side of the Pacific Bank is Murray's clothing store. It was here that Rowland Macy gave up storekeeping with his father, went whaling, became a "forty-niner," and later opened his own department store in New York City—R.H. Macy & Co.

Main Street Houses

Never a Captain grizzled and gray
Now climbs to the house-top walk,
Pipe and spyglass are put away:
But the wise ones sometimes talk
Of the pleasant ghosts that are peering still
Through the glasses out to sea
Thinking back to the lure of the ships
And the life that used to be.

—Mary Starbuck, *"The Walk"*

On upper Main Street and Pleasant Street are some very old houses and most of the elegant mansions that were built with whaling money. A good many of these houses are now owned by summer residents.

Nantucket's Historic District

Interest in preserving Nantucket's extraordinary architectural past has been occurring for years; in 1972 it was one of the first three communities in the country to set up an historic district. The plan was co-founded by Blair Reeves, Professor of Architecture at the University of Florida, and Walter Beinecke, who restored much of the waterfront.

Despite the fire that gutted the center of town in 1846, over 800 buildings predate the Civil War; it is the largest collection of authentic buildings in one community in the United States.

The preservation is a truly remarkable achievement and continues to the present. Preservation Institute: Nantucket, an organization associated with the University of Florida, sponsors an eight-week graduate program on the Island where the students study many areas of preservation. As Peter Prugh, the Director of the Preservation Institute, explained, "No place in the country has the kind of continuity of historic character that Nantucket does. No living, functioning town has ever been able to do what Nantucket has. We want to know how it works."

A truly English village, Nantucket's eighteenth- and nineteenth-century houses and elegant brick mansions are close together, right on the original cobblestoned streets, with deep gardens in the rear for privacy. Enclosed with intricately carved fences, roses tumbling over trellises, and old-fashioned English box hedges, the town is a village and a city, unique and unlike any other in the country.

As you will see, Nantucket is as famous for its exquisite architecture as it is for its whaling heritage. There are six identifiable styles from the 1600s to the Victorian period in the late nineteenth century. Certain features can help you identify these periods in Nantucket's architecture.

Both the Richard Garner House at 139 Main Street and the Oldest House are examples of the earliest seventeenth-century Medieval English cottages. These were followed by the traditional saltbox or lean-to house, which was shingled. In the third phase of design, the Double House had a raised rear wall, four bays, an off-center chimney, and usually a roof walk. There are many of these houses, which were built between 1750 and 1820. This was followed by the Federal-style house (1776–1830), which has chimneys on the end walls, delicate balustrades along the roof, sidelights and a fanlight around the front door, louvered shutters, and a cupola. The next phase, somewhat influenced by the Georgian mansions on the mainland, was a larger house also with chimneys on the end walls to allow for a central hall and symmetrical window and door placement. The Greek Revival style was prevalent in the mid-nineteenth century and is easily identifiable by Grecian columns and a portico. Nantucket was in a depression during the Victorian and Gothic Revival period, so there are very few of these buildings. The First Congregational Church is the town's outstanding example.

10. John Wendell Barrett House
72 Main Street

The white clapboard 1820 house at 72 Main Street was built by John Wendell Barrett, a successful whale oil merchant and president of the Pacific Bank. Notice the handsome Federal-period balustrade trim along the edge of the roof, high foundation, Greek Revival portico on the front, enclosed cupola, and glassed sidelights on either side of the six-panel door. Houses like this that combine two architectural styles are called transition houses.

11. Henry Coffin and Charles Coffin Houses
75 and 78 Main Street

Farther up the street, facing one another, are the Coffin brothers' handsome brick houses built in the early 1830s. Both men had inherited wealth and whaleships from their father. The structures are identical except that Charles, a Quaker, had somber brownstone trim around his front door and a plain walk on the roof, while Henry, who wasn't a Quaker, preferred more elegant white marble trim around his front door and a cupola. The brothers owned the whaleship *Constitution*, which was one of the first ships to use the camel to get over the bar and out of Nantucket Harbor. Both men were very civic-minded. Not only were they responsible for planting the elm trees on Main Street in 1851, but they also imported 40,000 pine trees, which they planted in the treeless outlying areas of the Island. In 1836 Charles and a friend, David Joy, gave the town the building that was the first Nantucket Library.

12. Mathew Crosby House
90 Main Street

The first owner of this handsome Federal house was a successful whaler and later a shipowner and merchant. Built in 1829, the building is graced with an exceedingly handsome fanlight over the six-panel front door. The door's sterling-silver knocker, doorknob, and nameplate display a certain elegance found in many of these larger homes. The structure is perfectly proportioned, with a handsome balustrade trim on the roof, two chimneys set in from the side walls, and double steps with gracefully curving handrail leading up to the front door. The elegant interior includes marble fireplaces and hand-blocked wallpaper.

13. The Three Bricks
93, 95, and 97 Main Street

Possibly the most famous houses in Nantucket, these three identical brick mansions were built between 1836 and 1838 by Joseph Starbuck for his three sons William, Matthew, and George. Patriarch of the Starbuck clan, Joseph had made millions with his whaleships. He built these three handsome houses for $54,000 but kept the title to the properties to make sure his sons would stay in the family business. Starbuck also built a whaleship called *Three Brothers*, which returned to Nantucket in 1859 after a five-year voyage with 6,000 barrels of oil, both feats being record making.

The houses are called East Brick, Middle Brick, and West Brick. They have identical porticos with black wrought iron fences, and their four chimneys are flush with the outside walls.

14. William Hadwen Houses
94 and 96 Main Street

ROB BENCHLEY

Joseph Starbuck also had three daughters, and they lived at 92, 96, and 100 Main Street, the area being a regular compound of wealthy merchants and their families. One daughter married William Hadwen, a native of Newport, Rhode Island, who came to the Island and worked as a silversmith. Later he operated the candle factory that is now the Whaling Museum. He engaged Frederick Brown Coleman, architect of the Baptist Church, to build his Greek Revival mansion and the one next door for his niece and adopted daughter, Mrs. George (Mary G. Swain) Wright.

The houses are nearly identical, although the columns on number 94, with its

One of the twin Hadwen mansions built in 1844–45 during the great whaling era. The most imposing Greek Revival houses in town, they are called the "Two Greeks" and are just across Main Street from the Starbucks' "The Three Bricks."

Corinthian capitals, are reputed to be copied from the portico of the "Tower of Winds" in Athens. A second-floor ballroom had a specially sprung dance floor and a rooftop dome that could be opened to the stars. Number 96, now owned by the Historical Association, is the only mansion open to the public. Built in 1845, the house is decorated with Federal, Empire, carved Italian marble fireplaces, and silver doorknobs; the interior shows how Nantucket's wealthy residents lived at the time. The historic gardens on the spacious lawn in the rear are maintained by the Nantucket Garden Club.

15. *Thomas Macy II House*
99 Main Street

What many consider the handsomest doorway in Nantucket adorns this white clapboard Federal house, which was built in 1770 and added on to in 1827. One of the earliest houses to show a big change from the stark, simple lines of the Quaker houses, this one was originally a typical four-bay (window) house, which Macy's father-in-law had purchased for $432. A former blacksmith, Macy became a successful shareholder in several whaling ships, and in the course of remodeling and enlarging his house, he kept the proportions beautifully in balance. He included many, rather than a few, of the adornments beginning to appear on Nantucket houses, and instead of looking cluttered, his house is striking.

Macy converted the house to a two-chimney residence with a central hall. The porch railing curves out from the door to the street and makes the front fence.

The front door itself is topped by a blind elliptical fanlight (wooden rather than glass); there are fluted columns on either side of the door, flanked by sidelights (glass windows). An unusual feature is the second-story window over the front door, which also has sidelights. Notice the well-proportioned roof walk, which is not out of scale, although it runs almost the full length of the roof.

Thomas Macy Doorway
Many people consider the doorway on the Thomas Macy house at
99 Main Street to be the most handsome one in Nantucket.

16. Christopher Starbuck House
105 Main Street

A few houses were moved to this area from the original Sherburne settlement. The eastern section of the Christopher Starbuck House is thought to have been built in 1690 in Sherburne, while the western half dates from about 1715. It is a typical Nantucket lean-to with many features of the second stage in the development of Island houses. It has twelve-over-twelve windows and a very plain door with a five-pane light over it.

17. Zaccheus Macy House
107 Main Street

While the Coffins and Starbucks accounted for thirteen of Main Street's handsome houses, the Macys were not far behind with five homes in the area to their credit (numbers 77, 86, 89, 99, and 107).

Typical of many Nantucket houses built at this time, this 1748 silvery grey–shingled, five-bay house has twelve-over-twelve windows, a very plain front door, and a picket fence. The fence gives an aesthetic touch as it ties one building to another, although it was built originally for the very practical purpose of keeping animals out. Although Zaccheus was a prominent merchant and boat builder, he is best remembered for his medical ability to set broken bones, a favorite hobby that, fortunately for his patients, he had studied in his youth. It is estimated that he set more than 2,000 in his lifetime, all free of charge. He was extremely well liked, a staunch friend of the Indians, and a noted historian.

18. Richard Gardner House
139 Main Street

Richard Gardner's father came to the Island in 1666, and this shingled, second-generation house (meaning it was built by the son of an original settler) is dated around 1690. It is an excellent example of a very early house. The lean-to added to the side of the house is most unusual. Because of the chimney's location, it is assumed that the original owner planned to extend the house as it has been built. Its heavy door with long, black, iron hinges, heavy beams, walls insulated with mud and wattle, oblong, diamond-shaped pane windows, and massive, off-center chimney give it many of the characteristics of a medieval cottage.

19. William Crosby House
1 Pleasant Street

You are now at the Civil War Monument, which is in the

middle of the street. Turn back toward town, on Main Street, and take your first right onto Pleasant Street. The handsome Greek Revival home, built in 1847, has a high foundation, large French windows, double parlors, silver doorknobs, marble mantels, and hand-blocked wallpaper.

When he had the house built, Crosby was a prosperous young whaling merchant married to the daughter of whaling Captain Seth Pinkham. Known for their attractive social gatherings, the Crosbys introduced frozen mousse to their friends and imported the first Chickering piano with which to entertain. Unfortunately this lifestyle was not to last, for the fire of 1838 that swept the wharf destroyed a huge amount of oil that Crosby had stored, and he suffered heavy losses. He survived this, only to have almost all of his holdings go up in flames in the fire of 1846, and the Crosbys were forced to sell their house.

20. Walter Folger House
8 Pleasant Street

The owner of this unpretentious house was the Island's genius in the early nineteenth century. Walter Folger was a mathematician, state senator, and U.S. congressman as well as a fine mechanic and inventor of an astronomical clock, now displayed in the Fair Street Museum. This extraordinary clock not only indicates the seconds, minutes, and hours of the day and the days of the month, but it also shows the phases of the moon, the positions of the sun, and the height of the tide in the Nantucket Harbor! A self-taught lawyer, teacher, and historian, Walter also studied medicine, learned French in order to study the European philosophers and scientists, and learned astronomy from a French treatise on the subject brought to the Island by a shipwrecked French sailor. His telescope was one of the finest, and he managed to discover spots on Venus other recognized scientists had missed. He also, at one time, had a successful factory for spinning and weaving cotton and wool. Walter was considered as "odd as huckleberry chowder," which isn't surprising, as his crowded mind was undoubtedly distracted from life's mundane things.

Richard Gardner House
The Richard Gardner House at 139 Main Street is one of the Island's oldest surviving houses. Note the lean-to design and the windows, which were imported from England.

Walter Folger House
Walter Folger always lived in this simple, but handsome, typical four-bay Quaker house at 8 Pleasant Street.

Moor's End
This beautiful Georgian-style brick mansion with its handsome brick wall enclosing a garden is thought to be Nantucket's most magnificent house. Located at 19 Pleasant Street, it was the first major brick mansion built on the island, and others soon followed.

Other outstanding members of this family included Abiah, Benjamin Franklin's mother; Charles, a noted New York lawyer who ran against Grover Cleveland for governor of New York; Peter, one of the ablest of the original settlers; and James A. Folger, who went to the West Coast and founded the Folger Coffee Company.

21. Moor's End
19 Pleasant Street

This enormous, Georgian-style brick mansion at the corner of Mill Street is considered by many to be Nantucket's most magnificent house. Built between 1829 and 1834 by Jared Coffin, who had acquired a fortune through his partnership in three successful whaleships, it has the grandeur of an English manor house. It is famous for its massive, brick-walled garden and the whaling murals on the dining room walls. Despite its elegance, the house did not satisfy Coffin's wife, who wanted

African Meeting House

Built in the 1820s at the corner of Pleasant and York Streets (a few blocks beyond Moors End), this old post-and-beam building was a church, a school for African American children, and a meeting house.

Although the first Africans to come to the Island were slaves, by the late 1770s there were very few of them still in bondage due to the strong influence of the Quaker religion. Quakers staunchly opposed slavery. Historical information about this group and their descendants is unknown, but the forebears of the present group were Cape Verdeans recruited as crewmen on American whaleships when they stopped at this Portuguese colony off the northwest coast of Africa. This section of town was originally called New Guinea, where Portuguese and African cultures mixed. Many of these crewmen became excellent whalers. The meeting house has been restored and is now a museum.

African Meeting House on Nantucket, circa 1827.

FREDERICK G. S. CLOW

to be closer to town; so he built the three-story Jared Coffin House at the corner of Broad and Centre streets. Moor's End was sold and resold several times before 1873, when Jared Gardner bought it at auction for $2,350.

22. Baptist Church
Summer Street and Trader's Lane

Turn back toward Main Street; your second right is Summer Street, and the Baptist Church is on your left. This handsome building was built in 1840, further evidence of the decline of the Quaker religion at that time.

23. St. Paul's Episcopal Church
Fair Street

Continue straight ahead and directly in front of you at the end of the block is the Island's Episcopal Church. The first church, a wooden structure built in 1838 on Broad Street, was destroyed in the great fire. St. Paul's Episcopal Church was built in 1902 and is noted for its Tiffany windows.

24. Quaker Meeting House
Fair Street

Bear left to head back toward Main Street and on your left is the Quaker Meeting House. Built in 1846, this stark, grey, rectangular building is the only Quaker meetinghouse left on the Island. Meetings, open to the public, are still held in this building in the summer months.

25. Fair Street Museum
Fair Street

Next to the meetinghouse is the Fair Street Museum, another Historical Association exhibit. The admission fee is $3.00.

The artists John Singleton Copley, Gilbert Stuart, Childe Hassam, Eastman Johnson, Theodore Robinson, and Tony Sarg all visited and painted Nantucket. The Fair Street Museum has become the Historical Association's art museum, and the rotating exhibits of historical paintings by contemporary artists, as well as nineteenth-century paintings and primitives, are beautifully displayed and well worth a visit. It also houses the Artists Association permanent collection.

26. *Unitarian Universalist Church or*
Old South Tower
Orange Street

Continue along Fair Street until you reach Main Street; turn right and then take your first right onto Orange Street. Over a 100-year period this street, with its fine view of the harbor, was the home of 126 whaling captains. Directly on your right is the Old South Tower, which was built in 1809. Although it was originally a Congregational Church, the parishioners gradually became more liberal and embraced Unitarianism. Pew ownership was bought, sold, and auctioned like real

Comet Hale-Bopp and the Unitarian Church.

Unitarian Universalist Church
One of Nantucket's most beautiful historic buildings, this famous landmark has magnificent trompe l'oeil paneling and a Goodrich organ, installed in 1831.

The Town Crier, 1892
A self-appointed town crier, Billy Clark picked up his news flashes
from the Unitarian Church's Old South Tower, where he watched
for incoming ships, fires, or any other unusual activity.

Church Bells

Many visitors are very curious about the bell ringing that goes on at the Unitarian Church's Old South Tower. Three times a day the town clock chimes fifty-two times. The tradition began in the 1930s; ringing the bell for three minutes took fifty-two chimes. This was done just before 7:00 A.M. to wake Islanders for work, at noon to signal lunch, and at 9:00 P.M. to get people off the streets.

estate. Rich in Island history, this famous landmark has recently undergone a complete structural restoration and had its golden dome, visible from far at sea, restored. The magnificent organ, built by William Marcellus Goodrich in 1831, is made of mahogany and ivory. The beautiful *trompe l'oeil* painting was done by the Swiss artist Carl Wendte in 1844. The church also established the town's first lending library and its first Sunday School.

The renowned clock tower was used by the town crier as well as by watchmen scanning the horizon for incoming ships or the ever-feared peril of fire. The church's bell strikes the hours, and at 7:00 A.M., noon, and 9:00 P.M. it strikes an additional fifty-two times. It was supposed to be rung for three minutes at those hours, but it was easier to count the strikes than to time them.

The tower was also very useful to Billy Clark, the most colorful of Nantucket's many town criers. He would climb the tower to scan the water for an incoming steamer, and if he saw one, he'd thrust his tin horn through the slats of the belfry to announce the vessel's arrival. Then he'd hurry on down to the waterfront to see what news he could pick up. Tooting his horn and ringing his bell to attract attention, he'd wander the streets calling out the latest news items from the mainland, as well as the coming events in town and the latest sales in the local stores. He once announced President Garfield's assassination and a party at the new roller-skating rink all in the same sentence!

This is the last stop on Tour I. Return to Main Street.

10

TOUR II: THE OUTSKIRTS OF TOWN

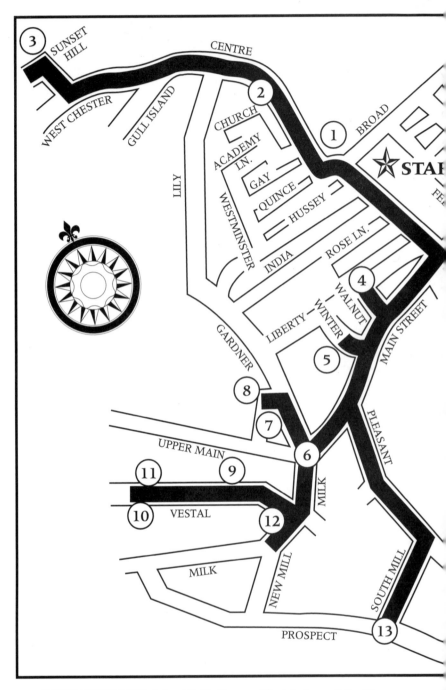

POINTS OF INTEREST: *1. Jared Coffin House and Captain George Pollard House*
2. Congregational Church and Old North Vestry 3. Jethro Coffin Hous.
4. Nathaniel Macy–Christian House 5. Sir Isaac Coffin School

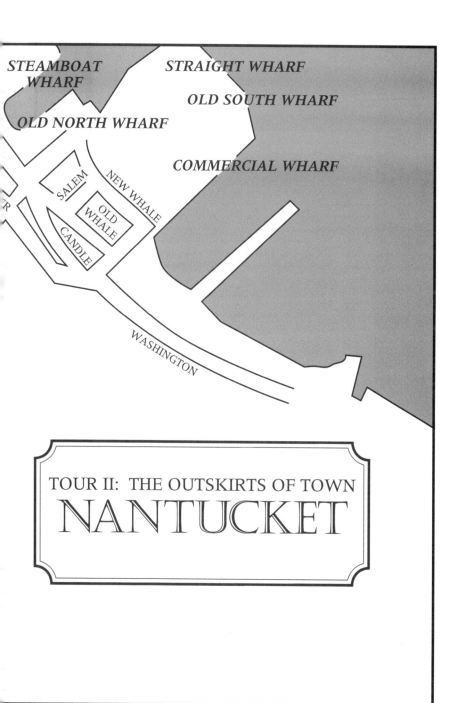

STEAMBOAT WHARF

STRAIGHT WHARF

OLD SOUTH WHARF

OLD NORTH WHARF

COMMERCIAL WHARF

SALEM

NEW WHALE

OLD WHALE

CANDLE

WASHINGTON

TOUR II: THE OUTSKIRTS OF TOWN

NANTUCKET

6. *Civil War Monument* 7. *Old Fire Hose Cart House* 8. *Greater Light*
9. *Maria Mitchell Birthplace and Library.* 10. *Cooperage* 11. *Old Gao*
12. *Hinchman House* 13. *Old Mill*

If you have the time, this tour covers the interesting land-
marks and Historical Association exhibits on the fringes of
town. These can be reached by a long, but very worthwhile,
walk, or by bike or car.

1. Jared Coffin House and
Captain George Pollard House
Corner of Centre and Broad streets

Next to the Pacific Bank on upper Main Street, turn right
onto Centre Street. During the whaling era this street was
called Petticoat Row because women managed all the shops
while their husbands were at sea. Three blocks over, where
Centre meets Broad Street, is the Jared Coffin House, which
has been an inn almost from its construction in 1845. Jared
Coffin had built this three-story house (one of the few on the
Island) for his wife, who had disliked the magnificent Moor's
End mansion that he had built for her. His wife was still dis-
satisfied, and the following year the Coffins moved to Boston.
Built of English brick with a Welsh slate roof and furnished
with lovely antiques, the Coffin house is a well-known
Nantucket landmark.

Diagonally across the street from the Coffin house is the
Seven Seas Gift Shop, which was Captain George Pollard's former home. There are many dramatic stories of tragedy and
success in whaling, but none surpasses the story of Captain
Pollard and his whaleship *Essex,* which was rammed and sunk
by a whale in 1820. The crew took to their open whaleboats

and drifted across the Pacific Ocean for three months. Only eight of the original twenty men survived, and this they accomplished by eating the flesh of their comrades. In such instances, usually the victim was chosen by drawing straws or the equivalent, although the cabin boy was often the first to go. In this case, the cabin boy was Captain Pollard's nephew, and they ate him first. Captain Pollard went to sea again, only to be shipwrecked once more. He finally gave it up and settled down for good on the Island, becoming a night watchman.

It was the tragic story of Captain Pollard and his ship, the *Essex,* that Herman Melville heard about in New Bedford and used as the basis for his famous novel *Moby Dick.* He drew on his own experiences aboard the Edgartown whaleship *Achusnet* under a cruel, demanding captain (the model for Captain Ahab) as well. A year after finishing the book, Melville made his first visit to Nantucket. He was walking up Centre Street with a friend toward the Coffin house when he noticed through the thick fog a man coming out of the Pollard house with a watchman's lantern. Pollard raised the lantern as he moved down the steps and Melville caught a glimpse of the old man's face.

"Who is that man?" he asked his companion, and he must have been quite overwhelmed. Later, Melville remarked on this dramatic encounter: "To the Islanders he was a nobody, but to me, the most impressive man, the most wholly unassuming—even humble that I ever encountered."

2. Congregational Church and Old North Vestry
62 Centre Street

Continue on Centre Street a few more blocks, and on your left is the huge, handsome, Gothic Revival Congregational Church built with whaling money in 1834. The trompe l'oeil painting and huge brass chandelier, 7 feet wide and more than 600 pounds in weight, enhance this striking building. Behind the church is the old vestry built in 1725. A small fee is now charged for the visitor to go up in the church tower for a spectacular view of the town and Island.

3. Oldest House or Jethro Coffin House
Sunset Hill Lane

Continue on Centre Street out of town, bearing to the left (Centre becomes West Chester Street) until you come to Sunset Hill Lane on your right and the Jethro Coffin house. It was built in 1686, and historians debate whether it's the oldest house on the Island. The house was a wedding present for Jethro Coffin and his bride, Mary Gardner, from their fathers. The timbers for the houses came from land in New Hampshire belonging to Jethro's father.

The house is a perfect example of a seventeenth-century house. The prominent features in this handsome building are the steep shed roof, heavy rough-hewn door, massive beams, small, diamond-shaped windows, "Indian closet," and huge center chimney with a horseshoe design on the front. There have been many theories about this design on the chimney. Some believe it might have been an antiwitch device, as the house was built at the same time as the Salem witch hunts; others think it might have been symbolic of the union of two principal families of the full-share and half-share factions; still others see the horseshoe as a good-luck symbol, although this one is upside down. The house is a Historical Association exhibit, and the admission fee is $1.00.

4. Nathaniel Macy–Christian House
26 Liberty Street

Returning to the center of town, go to the top of Main Street's square by the bank and continue up Main Street 1 block. Turn right onto Walnut Lane and at the corner of Liberty is this 1723 house built by Nathanial Macy, the grandson of the first white settler. This handsome five-bay house is typical of the stark simplicity of many Quaker houses. It is open to the public from mid-June to mid-September.

Jethro Coffin House

The Jethro Coffin House on Sunset Hill Lane was built in 1686 and might be the oldest house on Nantucket Island.

Maria Mitchell Birthplace and Observatory

The Maria Mitchell Association includes the Loines Observatory on Milk Street Extension and the Maria Mitchell Birthplace and a library on Vestal Street.

The Old Gaol

For two centuries, until 1933, the jail often held debtors or sailors who had gotten into rough brawls down on the water-front.

Civil War Monument
The Civil War Monument on Upper Main Street lists the names of sixty-nine
Nantucket men who died in the War Between the States.

5. Sir Isaac Coffin School
Winter Street

Return to Main Street on Walnut, turn right, and take the next right at Winter Street. A short distance on the left is Sir Isaac Coffin School. Sir Isaac was raised in Boston, served in the British Royal Navy, and remained a Loyalist during the Revolution. He was always an independent Nantucketer at heart however. He was a direct descendant of Tristram Coffin. After Sir Isaac retired and moved to Nantucket, he wanted to contribute something of lasting value to the Island. He had no children of his own but was persuaded to found a school for Coffin children, of whom there were a great many. Nantucket had no public education in those days, only Cent Schools. Parents paid a penny a day to have a child attend classes in one of several homes to learn reading and writing. The first Coffin School was founded on Fair Street, before this handsome brick building with its Doric columns was erected in 1852. Now the building houses the Eagan Institute of Marine Studies, a learning and resource center.

6. Civil War Monument

Return to Main Street, turn right to the Civil War Monument. This monument was erected in 1874 and is inscribed with the names of sixty-nine soldiers and sailors who lost their lives in the war.

7. Old Fire Hose Cart House
Gardner Street

Pass the Civil War Monument, and go right on Gardner Street. A short distance ahead on your left is a small building housing some of the earliest fire-fighting equipment, including a hand pumper and some handsome leather fire buckets.

8. Greater Light
8 Howard Street

Just beyond the Old Fire Hose Cart House on the left is Howard Street. Here is an old converted barn, named the Greater Light, which is the most unusual exhibit of the Historical Association. The decorative arts in the house are not just early American or China Trade, but rather a broad collection from Italy, Europe, and the Near East. There is an attractive brick patio, sunken yard, and basement dining room. The admission charge is $3.00.

9. Maria Mitchell Birthplace and Library
Vestal Street

Return again to the Civil War Monument and go up Milk Street, turning right into Vestal Street. Here on your right and across the street are the birthplace, library, and observatory of Maria Mitchell, a truly unusual Nantucket lady. Her father, William Mitchell, was a teacher, mathematician, astronomer, and bank cashier. Maria often helped him in "rating" chronometers for shipmasters and making observations of the stars with his telescope. Although her father had never attended college, this remarkable man became an overseer at Harvard College.

One fall evening in 1849, while scanning the heavens from her father's small observatory on the roof of the Pacific Bank, Maria discovered a comet. It became known to the outside world, and for her discovery and other work she was later awarded a gold medal from the king of Denmark. Although her education had been limited to Nantucket schools, Maria became a professor of astronomy at Vassar College for the second half of the nineteenth century. She became the first woman member of the American Academy of Arts and Sciences and the recipient of many honors. (It's not surprising that she was related to the brilliant Folger family.)

Maria's descendants, admirers, and former students founded the Maria Mitchell Association in her honor.

It includes the Loines Observatory, the Maria Mitchell Birthplace, a library, and the natural science center at the

Hinchman House (Maria's family's first house). The Loines Observatory on Milk Street Extension (on the way to Hummock Pond Road) is open to the public every Wednesday night during the summer.

10. Cooperage
Vestal Street

Farther along Vestal Street on the left is the remaining cooperage on the Island. When whaling was in its prime, there were many, many shops like this, where large and small whale oil casks were made. The wood from the tupelo trees that grow on the Island was very hard and good for making bungs to plug up the barrels. Today this building is a private residence.

11. Old Gaol
Vestal Street

Continuing along Vestal Street you'll see the old jail on your right. Constructed of oak logs bolted with iron, sheathed with pine, and shingled, the building has four cells with iron bars on small windows. Two of the cells have fireplaces, and one is sheathed on the inside with iron for the more dangerous criminals, although in two centuries of Island history there were not many.

12. Hinchman House
7 Milk Street

Backtrack to Milk Street, and at the corner of Milk and Vestal is the Natural Science Museum, called the Hinchman House, run by the Maria Mitchell Association. There are displays of the Island's flora and fauna, live snakes, and stuffed birds in this handsome early nineteenth-century house. The museum sponsors nature and bird walks, as well as seminars and workshops for adults and children.

13. Old Mill
South Mill Street

Return to Main Street, bear right 1 block to Pleasant Street, and continue along Pleasant until you come to the junction with South Mill Street. Bear right 1 long block. The Old Mill that stands here, built in 1746, is one of the oldest, if not the oldest, mills in the country. In continuous use since its completion, the mill is operated entirely by wind power. The original wooden machinery and millstone are still in good working condition, and corn milled on-site is sold at the mill during the summer. There were once four mills in this elevated area, and when Nantucket was caught up in two wars, the mills were sued for signaling ships offshore that were attempting to come into Nantucket Harbor. A Historical Association exhibit, the mill's admission fee is $1.00.

Cemeteries

For those interested in looking at old gravestones, there are five cemeteries on this southwest side of town. The Friends Cemetery is at the junction of Madaket Road and Quaker Road by Caton Circle. The stones here are recent, as Nantucket history goes, because for 150 years Quaker tradition forbid any headstones. Those you see in the northeastern section date from the final decades of Quakers on Nantucket.

Old New England Cemeteries

Old New England cemeteries often reveal the character of its townspeople. An old Nantucket epitaph illustrates the Yankee attitude of "show me and prove it":

"To follow you I'm not intent
Until I know which way you went."

The comet Hale-Bopp streaking over the Old Mill, which was used to signal ships during the Revolutionary and Civil Wars. The mill still provides cornmeal to the public.

A half mile beyond this is the Abiah Folger Franklin boulder and plaque in memory of Benjamin Franklin's mother, who was born near this site. The Prospect Hill Cemetery is bounded by Hummock Pond Road, Cato Lane, and Milk Street Extension. The Old South Cemetery, with many very early gravestones, is next to the Middle School on Atlantic Avenue. Another cemetery is behind the Cottage Hospital, and St. Mary's Roman Catholic Cemetery borders Prospect Street. On the far side of the Quaker Cemetery, at the corner of New Lane and West Chester Extension, is the Old North Burying Ground, which also has some very old headstones.

FREDERICK G. S. CLOW

Nantucket Life Saving Museum at Folger's Marsh, Polpis.

11

Tour III: The Outlying Areas

TOUR III: THE OUTLYING AREAS
NANTUCKET

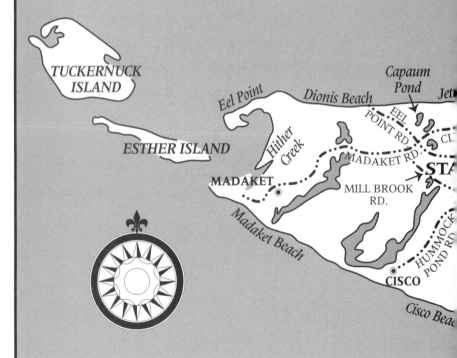

TUCKERNUCK ISLAND

ESTHER ISLAND

Eel Point

Dionis Beach

Capaum Pond

Jet

EEL POINT RD.

Hither Creek

CL

MADAKET RD.

STA

MADAKET

MILL BROOK RD.

Madaket Beach

HUMMOCK POND RD.

CISCO

Cisco Bea

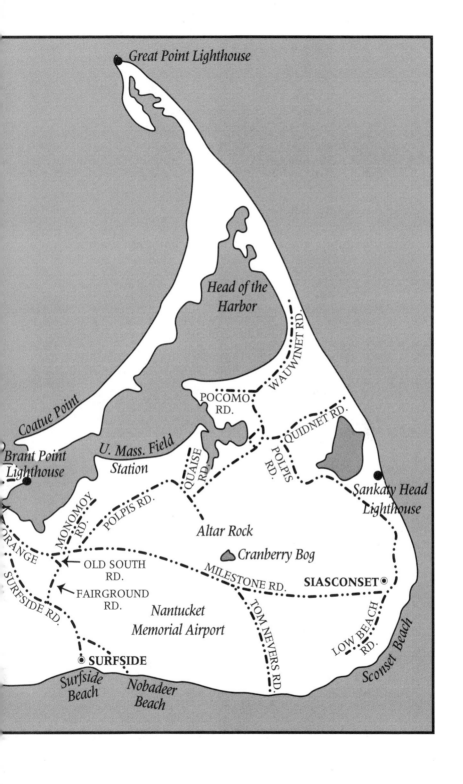

Great Point Lighthouse

Head of the
Harbor

WAUWINET RD.

Coatue Point

POCOMO
RD.

QUIDNET RD.

Brant Point
Lighthouse

U. Mass. Field
Station

QUAISE RD.

POLPIS
RD.

Sankaty Head
Lighthouse

MONOMOY RD.

POLPIS RD.

Altar Rock

Cranberry Bog

ORANGE

OLD SOUTH
RD.

MILESTONE RD.

SIASCONSET

SURFSIDE RD.

FAIRGROUND
RD.

Nantucket
Memorial Airport

TOM NEVERS RD.

LOW BEACH RD.

SURFSIDE

Surfside
Beach

Nobadeer
Beach

Sconset Beach

These areas out from the town of Nantucket contain little pockets of settlements along the Island's perimeter, both on the harbor side and on the eastern and southern shores of the Island. There are fingerlike coves reaching in from the sea that are fringed with green ribbons of marsh to provide small harbors in several places along the south shore. The low, rolling moors are dotted with weathered, grey-shingled houses and winding, narrow dirt roads criss-cross the area. There are paved roads to all the principal settlements.

The large, open areas were made possible by the tireless work of many to conserve as much property as possible. Now more than one-third of Nantucket is protected from further development by private, state, or federal organizations. These large tracts of land help to maintain the delicate balance between humans and nature and are critical to the Island's survival, and their naturalness is a contrast to the massive construction and building that goes on elsewhere.

The Island's 10,000 acres of moors with low-growing vegetation—bright, yellow Scotch broom, bayberry beach plum, grape, holly, heather, huckleberry, bearberry—and hundreds of wildflowers blanket these areas. So far, no squirrel, chipmunk, raccoon, fox, weasel, skunk, porcupine, or muskrat has found its way to the Island, although deer, pheasant, and cottontail rabbits abound and can be seen on nature walks. Birds of all kinds are everywhere.

Monomoy

The tour begins in a clockwise direction, taking Orange Street, which is a left turn off Main Street, 4 blocks up from the foot of the town square at the Pacific Club. Orange Street

Harbor seals are seen year-round on the island.

leads out to a rotary with signs pointing to Siasconset (always called 'Sconset) and Polpis. Bear left on Polpis Road, and follow it a very short distance to Monomoy Road on the left. Turn here, and after a short distance Monomoy dead-ends at a cluster of houses east of the town of Nantucket. You will have a fine view across the harbor to the town.

Residents living here in these handsome, grey-shingled houses belong to some of the oldest summer families, along with those in the Cliff area near Jetties Beach. They acquired summer homes here before World War I; the next wave of summer residents bought in town after World War II.

Life Saving Museum
Polpis Road

Return to Polpis Road and bear left. Two miles farther along is an original Life Saving Museum, which was built at Surfside in 1874. Picture if you can this crescent-shaped dollop of land in the Atlantic, which Daniel Webster called that "city in the sea," with shifting sands and currents swirling all around it. To protect or rescue those manning the hundreds

The artifacts at Nantucket Life Saving Museum provide a fascinating glimpse of Nantucket's maritime history.

of vessels sailing in the area, there were the lightships positioned offshore and before them "humane" houses at the most vulnerable points around the Island's shores. Here, men would be on the lookout for vessels in distress, and there were many of them. Finally they built lifesaving stations at strategic points around the Island.

The museum has two early lifesaving boats, a breeches buoy, quarterboards, lightship displays, and other equipment used by the heroic men who put out in any weather to rescue survivors of wrecked vessels. It is open from mid-June through September.

The Nantucket Shoals

From early days to the present time, the raging seas surrounding Nantucket continue to claim lives and vessels. In 1956 treacherous fogs, like a shroud enveloping the Atlantic, claimed the liner *Andria Doria* when she collided with the Swedish liner, the *Stockholm,* 60 miles south of the Island; the *Andria Doria* went to the bottom on the Nantucket shoals. Response to the disaster was immediate, and many of those injured were flown to Nantucket's hospital. All Islanders rushed to help in whatever way they could.

Unfortunately, the *Doria* continues to claim lives—ten divers so far, three in the summer of 1988. They continue to find the challenge to explore the sunken vessel irresistible despite the currents, the darkness, and the blue sharks that circle around as they return to the surface slowly to avoid getting the bends. One experienced diver, who didn't surface in the allotted time, was found dead in the first-class bar 200 feet below the surface.

Despite modern technology, the shoals continue to claim ships, and twenty years after the *Andria Doria* went down in 1976, the oil tanker, the *Argo Merchant,* ran aground in a winter storm, releasing millions of gallons of fuel oil. The damage to fish and wildlife was somewhat minimized by offshore winds, and there was no loss of life.

Field Station
University of Massachusetts

Just a short distance beyond the museum, on the left, is the road into the University of Massachusetts's Nantucket Field Station. The field station serves as a base for presentation of undergraduate and graduate courses in the natural sciences (field biology, geology, and anthropology) and in the arts and humanities. Courses are offered year-round and are open to Nantucket residents as well as mainland students. Although the station has no public exhibits or facilities and is not open to the public, interested persons may call for an appointment to visit the station. The telephone number is (508) 228–5268.

Quaise
Quaise Road

Continuing on toward Polpis, the area on your left is Quaise, which is about midway along Nantucket Harbor. Historically it is worth noting this was the area that Thomas Mayhew kept when he sold the rest of the Island to the nine original purchasers. It was once the site of an insane asylum that burned to the ground and at another time the home of Keziah Coffin, a devout Loyalist. During the Revolution she carried on a monopoly in trade between Nantucket and New York under the protection of the British Navy when the Americans were prohibiting exports to the Island. A very shrewd and independent woman, Keziah was thoroughly disliked, although Nantucketers were totally dependent on the merchandise she had for sale. After the war, residents joined forces to bring about the collapse of her vast real estate holdings.

Altar Rock

Just opposite the dirt road into Quaise is a dirt road leading to Altar Rock, 90 feet above sea level and reported to be the highest point on the Island. It is a very short distance off the main road, and one can walk a bike in easily. On a summer day, the view from here of the green, flower-splashed moors, the deep blue of the sea, and the silhouette of the town against a clear sky is well worth the stop.

Great Point Lighthouse
*The 166-year-old Great Point Lighthouse was demolished by a
storm in March 1984. A replica made of rubblestone was complet-
ed in 1986. Set back from the shore, it is partially powered by
solar energy.*

Polpis

Continue on Polpis Road. In a short distance there is a rough dirt road on your left leading into Polpis Harbor. There are only private homes on it. In the seventeenth century Polpis was the most successful farming community on the Island. It was also the site of fulling mills, where sheep's wool was processed into cloth. Peat digging for fuel was carried on in this area as well as salt making. This was done by evaporating seawater in large vats. The salt was used not only for regular cooking but also to preserve fish. The peaty bottoms of former ponds in the area now nourish beech, maple, oak, and the Oriental-looking tupelo trees as well as ferns, holly, and sassafras.

Nantucket Island School of Design and the Arts
Wauwinet Road

Return to the main road and just ahead, located in an old dairy barn just before the junction of the Polpis and Wauwinet roads, is the School of Design. Open year-round, it offers graduate and undergraduate credit courses through the Massachusetts College of Art. An excellent selection of lectures and workshops in advanced painting, sculpture, figure painting, photography, underwater photography, textiles, videography, art history, basket weaving, and other subjects are offered.

Pocomo
Pocomo Road

Continuing on toward Wauwinet, go left on Wauwinet Road and left again on Pocomo Road, which is paved for quite some distance before it becomes a hard-to-manage dirt road. From the paved road you can get a fine view of the upper part of Nantucket Harbor. A century ago a favorite pastime of visitors to Nantucket was to take a catboat from the town to Pocomo or Wauwinet for "bathing"—one never used the term "swimming" in those days—and a noon picnic. The Pocomo beach, with its crystal-clear water and gentle sandy beach, was a favorite spot for years.

Wauwinet
Wauwinet Road

Return to Wauwinet Road, go left, and in a short distance you'll come to a halt at an information booth. Unless you have a jeep and a permit to explore the area or a house just beyond the hotel, you won't be able to see the head of the harbor. This spot is the gateway to the long, thin barrier beach—the whale's tail—that stretches out to the tip at Great Point and curls around to Coatue, the scalloped barrier beach that forms Nantucket Harbor.

Just beyond the tiny summer colony, which is nestled in a grove of Japanese black pines, and the lovely, Victorian Wauwinet Inn, is the Haulover. Years ago, fishermen used to haul their dories over the sandbar (hence, Haulover) to get into Nantucket Harbor without making the long trip around Great Point. Periodically the ocean breaks through, and then the beach builds up again, closing the opening. The last time the ocean broke through was in the spring of 1984.

Quidnet
Quidnet Road

Staying on the paved road, retrace your steps to the intersection of Polpis Road and bear left onto Quidnet Road, which dead-ends down at the beach. There are cottages here alongside the beach and Sesachacha Pond, but during the whaling and cod fishing era, when small boats went out from shore here, this was an active fishing village. The section of the barrier beach separating the pond from the ocean belongs to the Nantucket Conservation Foundation. The area is wild and undeveloped, and the huge, pink, four-petaled rose mallows growing around the pond are a lovely sight in midsummer.

Siasconset

Leaving Quidnet, head back to the paved Polpis Road and go left. This leads to 'Sconset. Opposite the Sankaty Head Golf Club, which is private, you will see the Sankaty Head Lighthouse on your left. It was these sandy cliffs that English explorer George Waymouth mentioned in 1604 while he was sailing offshore. The Sankaty Head light is visible 29 miles out at sea.

Siasconset was settled in the seventeenth century, and some of its tiny houses are the oldest on the Island. It's a village in miniature where doll-sized, weathered-grey cottages with sloping roofs are covered with rambler roses and hollyhocks fill their doorways. Nestled close together on this bluff of land overlooking the sea, the houses are separated by narrow, winding grass paths that enhance the Lilliputian character and charm of the community.

The cottages were first built as one-room fishing shacks by fishermen from town who came to 'Sconset to go offshore for shore whaling and cod fishing. They spent the season here, but eventually the wives decided they wanted to join their husbands, so "warts," or small bedrooms, were tacked onto the dwellings. They began enclosing the kitchen porches, which had wooden chimneys, and as time went on, other additions were added here and there, very casually. Below the town today is a beach area known as Codfish Park.

In the 1880s, Nantucket was having a welcome tourist boom, and wealthy residents from town started building summer homes on the edge of the 'Sconset settlement. In 1884 arrangements were made by the owners of the Nantucket Railroad to extend their track out to 'Sconset from Surfside. Their train, Dionis, was the pride of Nantucket; some years later it was succeeded by another train called 'Sconset. Heavy storms kept ruining the track that ran alongshore, so the route was changed to run directly from town out to 'Sconset. Then a new gasoline motor car called The Bug and the Bird Cage was put on the run. It flew over the tracks to 'Sconset in nineteen minutes and, unfortunately, became so frisky it plummeted off the road one day and was squashed. A successor managed to "turn turtle" on South Beach but was retrieved and continued in service for several years. Finally a

Nantucket Lightships

For three centuries the shallow sea surrounding the Island—those treacherous Nantucket shoals—has been a graveyard of ships. The shifting sands, the raging Northeasters, and the fog—often as thick as cotton batting—have claimed thousands of vessels and many lives. Tha ability to rescue those aboard ships in distress improved dramatically in 1901 when the Italian genius Guglielmo Marconi set up a wireless station, the first in America, at 'Sconset. It was able to transmit and receive messages from steamships crossing the Atlantic. These messages were relayed to the station via the famous Nantucket Lightships. In those days the arrival and departure of these elegant passenger liners was a major event.

Among the young men assigned to this isolated station in the early days was David Sarnoff. By 1914 he had been transferred to New York, and on the night of April 15th, Sarnoff picked up the S.O.S. from the Titanic. He immediately alerted the Eastern seaboard of the impending disaster and ships in the area responded. His handling of the crisis became a major news event. Many years later Sarnoff became Chairman of RCA.

new train, consisting of locomotive, passenger car, and baggage car, operated until 1917, when the railroad was abandoned.

Before the turn of the century, 'Sconset became a very popular summer colony for theater personalities from New York City, such as Lillian Russell and Joseph Jefferson. Fortunately they contributed to the preservation of the tiny houses, undoubtedly because of their limited financial means and because of their appreciation of the character of the village. They didn't mind standing in line at the old wooden pump to get their water; the pump, too, has been carefully preserved in the center of 'Sconset.

Marconi established a wireless station in 'Sconset, which was the first station to participate in reporting maritime news or transmitting calls for help in sea disasters. One of the young operators who worked here was David Sarnoff, who later went on to found RCA.

Auld Lang Syne in Siaconset was a fishing shack in the seventeenth century.

Codfish Park, below the bluff, is just north of the town's public beach, where there is a lifeguard on duty. In the center of the village by the rotary is a catering shop that puts up box lunches to take to the beach, a liquor store, a grocer, a post office, and a newspaper store. The 'Sconset Casino nearby is a private tennis club, which also shows movies that are open to the public, and the famous Chanticleer restaurant is here.

Ocean Avenue

Bear right at the little rotary in the center of the village of 'Sconset to take the road along the Atlantic Ocean. Go past the guidepost directing you to Spain, the next landfall to the east, and on to the large Coast Guard Station. Just as the road starts to curve around here, you are facing the south shore. ('Sconset faces east and, when the weather is bad, gets those northeasters head on.) The erosion here is so severe that several acres a year are lost.

Cranberry Bog
Milestone Road

Doubling back to the center of town, take Milestone Road (also called 'Sconset Road), which is the main road running from 'Sconset into town. A short distance along this road, on your right, is the dirt road leading into the cranberry bog that has been in existence since the seventeenth century. While cranberries had been used for years as a staple on sailing ships, it wasn't until the 1850s, after the whaling and sheep economies had declined, that they became a cash crop. The Nantucket Cranberry Company at one time had all 400 acres under cultivation, but by the 1960s low prices forced the owner to sell. Walter Beinecke, the late Roy Larsen (a summer resident and former president of Time, Inc.), and Arthur Dean (a New York lawyer) bought the bog and gave it to the Nantucket Conservation Foundation. Today about 100 acres are under cultivation, with plans for more, and the fruit is shipped to the Ocean Spray Company on Cape Cod. Beehives are placed near the bog to help with pollination; their honey is sold on the Island. Profits from the cranberries and honey

Cranberries are floated out of their bogs during the annual October harvest.

When the wind is up, surfboarding is very popular off Cisco and other beaches along the Island's south shore.

go to the Nantucket Conservation Foundation to help with its extraordinarily successful efforts to preserve the land. The bog is open for viewing, under certain restrictions, at harvesttime.

Just past the bog on the left is the road to Tom Nevers, which leads down to the shore and the site where the Carnival, County Fair, and other events take place.

Surfside
Surfside Road

Continue on Milestone Road toward town; just before the rotary turn left onto Old South Road and immediately bear right onto Fairgrounds Road. At the next intersection bear left onto Surfside Road, which leads on down to the ocean. The beautiful, broad, sandy beach is one of the most popular swimming spots on the Island.

Cisco
Hummock Pond Road

Return toward town on Surfside Road. Opposite the school on your right is Vesper Lane on your left. Take this road to Milk Street and go left again on Hummock Pond Road, which leads down to the popular beach at Cisco. The vast plains to your right, which Henry David Thoreau called "a prairie," were used for sheep grazing and were the site of the annual sheepshearing. There is a public golf course here. A sign shows the way to Bartlett's famous produce farm, which has been in business for years. The fall is so mild on Nantucket that crops that cannot grow on Martha's Vineyard or Cape Cod are available here. The produce-and-flower cart, which arrives every morning on the cobblestone square in the center of town and has been an Island institution for years, has an abundant selection in the late fall.

Madaket
Madaket Road

Return again toward town and take Millbrook Road to the left, which leads over to Madaket Road. A left turn leads the traveler down to this charming harbor on the western tip of the Island. At the end of the road is a fine public fishing area that is popular for catching bluefish. Once again, shifting sands have connected Nantucket and Esther Island, the original Old Smith Point before it was cut off by Hurricane Esther in 1971 and renamed. Return from the point on the road that runs alongside Hither Creek. The creek provides a fine, protected anchorage for small boats, and at its head is a boat yard. Grey seals from offshore swim up this creek to feed on the herring. Little Neck, on the north side of the creek on Madaket's crescent-shaped harbor, is owned by the Nantucket Conservation Foundation. Eel Point, on the northern side of Madaket Harbor, is another property of the Foundation. The currents swirling around the point make swimming very dangerous. There has been an enormous building boom here, and houses and cottage are available to rent. There are a large shipyard, grocer, and the Westender Restaurant here.

Dionis Beach
Eel Point Road

Return toward town on Madaket Road and turn left on the first paved road, clearly marked with a sign, to Dionis Beach. The paved road ends at the beach, which has lovely, rolling dunes and gentle surf because it faces Nantucket Sound.

Jetties Beach
North Beach Street

Leaving Dionis and heading back to Madaket Road, take the paved Cliff Road at the intersection to your left and continue back to town. This particular drive through open, rolling land offers beautiful vistas of the western end of the Island. You'll come to Macy's Pond on your right. The dirt road just beyond leads over to the Founding Father's Burying Ground. Some of Nantucket's most elegant summer houses are on the bluff overlooking Nantucket Sound in this area. Cliff Road leads to Easton Street; bear left and take your second left on North Beach Street. You double back here, heading out of town until you come to Jetties Beach. This is a large area with delightful swimming. Because it offers so many conveniences, it is extremely popular.

Brant Point

Leaving Jetties Beach, go left on Hulbert Avenue and follow it to the Brant Point Lighthouse. There have been several lighthouses on this site since the first one was built in 1746. The early lighthouse was a lantern hung between two poles.

Later lighthouses consisted of larger lanterns on top of a platform, until a regular lighthouse was finally built.

The beach area is small and lacks facilities because the currents can be quite strong. It is really best enjoyed as a spot from which to watch the boats going in and out of Nantucket Harbor.

Follow Easton Street back to town, past Children's Beach to the wharves.

12

SPECIAL EVENTS

To raise money for various organizations, Nantucketers have many auctions, antiques shows, fishing tournaments, and athletic events all summer long. There are also many lectures, concerts, art exhibits, plays, sporting events, and walking tours. The following is a brief list of some of these annual events.

April

Easter Sunday

Sunrise services are held at the Old Mill and at Altar Rock, the highest point on the Island.

Easter Egg Hunt

The chamber of commerce sponsors this event on Easter Sunday afternoon on the lawn of the Nantucket Cottage Hospital.

Daffodil Festival Weekend

It was in 1974 that Jean MacAusland, the wife of the publisher of *Gourmet* magazine, originated a Daffodil Exhibit with the Nantucket Garden Club. It gradually became a weekend festival. Now Nantucket annually celebrates the rites of spring the last weekend of April, and it is a great tribute to MacAusland. More than a million daffodils line the roadsides, and the town itself bursts into bloom. Prizes are awarded for the most attractive shop window. There's an Antique Car Parade, with autos decorated with daffodils, from town out to Siasconset for a Tailgate Picnic on Sunday (with Monday the rain date). On the weekend the American Daffodil Society, in conjunction with the Nantucket Garden Club, holds an exhibition and judging of flowers and arrangements at one of the hotels, there's a tour of inns, the Daffodil Ball, and an auction.

Library Open House

The Maria Mitchell Association Library, in observance of National Library Week, holds an annual open house to mark the end of winter. Exhibits show the early arrival of island birds, flowers, and plants as well as what constellations to look for in the spring sky.

Artists Association of Nantucket

Beginning the end of April, the Artists Association of Nantucket has a wealth of exhibits, several auctions, a benefit supper dance, and many workshops for adults and children; events continue into the fall. Call 228–0722 for details.

May

Bike and Road Races

Starting in May and lasting into the fall, the Nantucket Cycling Club sponsors many bike races. Check with them or with the Nantucket Information Bureau and the Chamber of Commerce about other sponsored races.

There are also many road races, from early spring to late fall.

The popular Daffodil Weekend in April includes an Antique Car Parade that terminates in 'Sconset where participants stage elaborate picnics.

NICOLE GRANT

Nantucket Wine Festival

This mid-May prelude to many summer events attracts wine experts from all over the world. While there is one very fine, small Nantucket vineyard, it is the extraordinary number of restaurants that have received the *Wine Spectator* magazine's top awards that has attracted these wine connoisseurs from around the world. There are wine tastings, delicious dinners, and lectures. It is a colorful event in the "shoulder season" when the Island is still quiet, restaurants are open, and the beaches are cool and empty. It's an ideal time for those who want to avoid the July and August crowds.

FREDERICK G. S. CLOW

The Figawi Boat Race from Hyannis to Nantucket, 1998.

The Nantucket Wine Festival

The three-day program of wine tastings, dinners, and parties takes place in mid-May. Because so many restaurants have award-winning selections of wine for their guests, it has become very popular.

Figawi Boat Race

This annual event takes place on Memorial Day weekend, and the boats race from Hyannis, on Cape Cod, to Nantucket. It has become a very popular party weekend and is limited to 200 boats.

Memorial Day Weekend

During this weekend, many homeowners return to open their houses for the summer, ferry reservations for a car are impossible unless they were made months in advance, and the hotels are filled. The annual "Hooked on Nantucket" Bluefish Tournament, windsurfer races, and golf tournaments are scheduled for the weekend.

June

Cranberry Classic Road Race

This annual event in mid-June is a roadrace for 300 joggers. It has become increasingly popular through the years. There are other road races all season, so check with the newspapers or the Nantucket Information Bureau for upcoming events.

Harborfest

This waterfront celebration the first weekend in June includes kayak clinics for adults and children, a Windsurfing Regatta, children's pirate parade, marine biology exhibits, games at Children's Beach, and other activities.

Nantucket Film Festival

Held for a week in mid-June, this festival has become an extremely popular, nationally known event.

Nantucket Film Festival

In 1996 Nantucket residents Jill Goode and her brother, Jonathan Burkhart, conceived the idea of a Nantucket Film Festival where screenwriters are honored and judged by the actors and directors. The festival's events include the showing of feature-length films, short subject films, lectures, staged readings, and panel discussions. At the conclusion of the festivities, there is a reception for an Audience Choice Award, the Tony Cox Award for screenwriting, and a Lifetime Achievement Award.

The festival has given some valuable exposure to many upcoming screenwriters. The 1997 low-budget festival film *The Full Monty* went on to become one of five Academy Award nominees. During the 1998 festival *Southie* was first shown and also became successful.

At the 1998 festival, Brad Anderson, who had just sold his movie *Next Stop Wonderland* at the Sundance Film Festival for $6,000,000, explained the importance of these festivals. "The best stuff out of Hollywood first saw the light of day in independent films. . . . A festival like Nantucket's didn't exist a few years ago, and now it's one of the most noticed in the country."

Some of the week's events are open to the public, including the films that are shown at the Gaslight and Dreamlight theaters.

Actor Ben Stiller signing autographs at the Nantucket Film Festival.

Matt Lauer, a Nantucket Film Festival favorite, and Al Roker of The Today Show.

Ring Lardner Jr., recipient of the Nantucket Film Festival's Lifetime Achievement Award in 1998, with Jerry Stiller, Brooke Shields, and Francis Lardner.

Celebrity Fishing Tournament

The annual John Havlicek Celebrity Fishing Tournament, held in late June, benefits the Genesis Fund to raise money for children with birth defects. Many sports celebrities participate.

Iron Man Race

The annual Nantucket Iron Man Race, which includes running, biking, and swimming, occurs in mid-June.

July

Fourth of July

There are children's playground games, a band concert, and fireworks at Jetties Beach. An afternoon watermelon eating contest at a long table on Main Street is followed by the traditional water fight, which the children love!

The Annual Firehouse Water Fight, July 4, 1998.

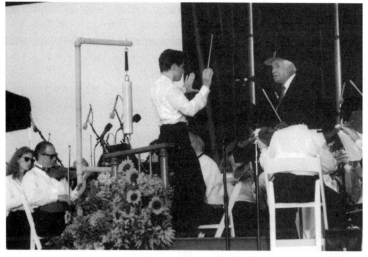

The Boston Pops, conducted by Keith Lockhart, with famed Red Sox announcer Curt Gowdy as a guest participant in a chorus of "Take Me Out to the Ball Game."

Flower Show

The Nantucket Garden Club has its annual Green Thumb and Flower Show in July at the Breeze Point Hotel on Easton Street. The public may participate.

Boston Pops

In mid-July the Boston Pops plays at Jettie's Beach. Thousands of people gather both on the beach and in boats that anchor offshore. The 1998 finale was the *1812 Overture*, played while fireworks exploded over the water!

Antiques Shows

Two annual antiques shows, which are held at the elementary school on Atlantic Avenue (the road to Surfside), are benefits for the Nantucket Historical Association and the Nantucket schools. Because there are so many fine antiques

Special Events **191**

shops on the Island, the selection at the show is excellent, and off-Island dealers also participate. They are held in July and August. There are others all summer long; they are well advertised in the newspapers.

Rose Sunday

In the very beautiful Congregational Church on Centre Street, the charming custom of Rose Sunday takes place. The inspiration of a former pastor, the event involves filling the church with roses—which thrive in Nantucket's warm winters, cool summers, and constant summer breezes that provide the necessary circulation—and holding a concert of choral music.

Carnival

The annual Carnival takes place in mid-July at Tom Nevers Head.

Billfish Tournament

The Nantucket Anglers' Club, a private fishing club, sponsors a tournament late July or early August that is open to the public. Limited to fifty boats, the sport fishermen go offshore for sailfish and marlin, and prizes are awarded.

Nantucket Tennis Classic

Some nationally known tennis stars play in this annual event held at the Brant Point Racquet Club in late July.

Swan Regatta

These beautiful sailboats gather for a three-day regatta the end of July.

Auction

The Artists Association of Nantucket holds two auctions in late July; a silent and live auction at the gallery and a live auction in a private home.

St. Pauls Church House and Garden Tour

Five lovely houses are open in mid-July, and refreshments are served at the Parish House.

August

Annual House Tour

The Nantucket Garden Club sponsors an annual house tour, which takes place in mid-August. The houses open for the tour are private homes, not those belonging to the Historical Association. Most of them are old, although some may be modern, and they are different each year. They are geographically grouped together, so one may take a cab or bus to a certain area, buy a ticket at the door of one of the houses, and easily walk to the others. The proceeds from this tour go to the garden club.

Nantucket Bucket Sail Race

This annual event of huge sailboats, many over 100 feet, is a two-day event held in Mid-August.

Antiques Shows

The original Nantucket Antique Show to benefit the Nantucket Fire Department and EMT Series is held at the Island Marine Service on Washington Street. The Nantucket

Historical Association show at Nantucket High School follows a few days later.

Annual Folk Art and Craft Show

There are many fine craftsmen on the Island, and this is a fine opportunity for them to display their work. Location varies.

Sand Castle Contest

The Chamber of Commerce and the Nantucket Island School of Design and the Arts sponsor this event each summer at Jetties Beach. It's extremely popular with children, but many adults also participate, creating large, fanciful sculptures that last until the incoming tide takes them away.

Opera House Cup Race

Held in mid-August, this annual ocean race for classic wooden-hulled sailboats only has become very popular. Maritime history buffs particularly enjoy seeing the harbor filled with these historic vessels, many of which formerly raced in the America Cup Series.

Tomato Cook-Off

The Great Tomato Cook-Off is at Bartlett's Farm, with Island chefs preparing tomatoes in many innovative ways.
A benefit for Small Friends on Nantucket.

Annual Tree Fund Reception and Dinner Party

The high school auditorium is the location of this unusual event now in its eighteenth year.

Annual Tree Fund Reception and Dinner Party

Not many places have parties for trees, but they have always been a special commodity on this windswept Island. Herman Melville called the Island "an elbow of sand" where "pieces of wood in Nantucket are carried about like bits of the true cross in Rome; . . . people there plant toadstools before their houses to get under the shade in the summertime. . . ." This fund is used primarily to replace those beautiful wineglass elms that have been killed by the Dutch Elm Disease.

The Broward Annual Rendezvous

Large private yachts gather for a three-day weekend the end of August.

September

Hurricane Cup Regatta

The annual Hurricane Cup Sailboat Regatta takes place in early September. To participate, call (800) NAN–BOAT.

Cottage Hospital Benefit

The annual Golf Tournament Benefit for the Nantucket Cottage Hospital is held at the Sankaty Head Golf Club in mid-September.

County Fair

Nantucket Island School of Design has a Kite Flying Contest, among other events at the fair in late September, held at Tom Nevers.

County Fair, held annually in late September at Tom Nevers.

October

Annual Arts Festival

Held in mid-October, this colorful fall event includes performances and exhibitions in drama, music, film, textile arts, and literature. The Artist's Association Auction occurs at this time.

Columbus Day Road Race

Columbus Day is another very big weekend on Nantucket, since it is the end of the season for many people. Organized by various sponsors, this 10-mile road race starts at Siasconset Village, runs over the Polpis Road, and finishes at the Nantucket Boys Club on Sparks Avenue. There are five divisions of runners.

Cranberry Harvest Weekend

The following week, an increasingly popular annual celebration of the cranberry harvest includes a guided tour of the bogs, cookery contest, and craft exhibitions, an inn tour, and window decorating contest.

November

Nantucket Noel

The holiday season begins on Thanksgiving weekend, which has become one of the Island's busiest times; hotels and inns are filled and dinner reservations should be made weeks in advance. The town highway department raises the bricks along Main Street from the Pacific Bank down to the waterfront and plants live Christmas trees the whole length of both sides of the street. They are all decorated by schoolchildren, who use everything from cranberries to painted scalloped shells as ornaments, and they are lit on Friday. Visitors are set back a century or more as they look up the street at this charming nineteenth-century scene. Only the electricity seems to be a twentieth-century intrusion. The pealing of church bells completes this delightful picture.

December

Christmas Shoppers Stroll

It has been two decades since the first Christmas Shoppers Stroll, held annually on the first Saturday in December. The influx of people to this holiday setting, which looks like a Charles Dickens Christmas card, increases every year. Everyone seems to want to join in to make it a very festive event. Carolers' voices ring out the glad tidings from the steps of the bank at the top of the square, roasted chestnuts are offered by the Boy Scouts, there are wandering minstrels and hot mulled cider, and Santa and Mrs. Claus arrive by horse-drawn sled or wagon. The streetlamps lining the cobblestone square are decked out in pine and red ribbons. A house tour is held, with six historical houses beautifully decorated for the holidays.

Community Christmas Celebration

The Christmas Pageant at the strikingly beautiful Congregational Church on the Sunday before Christmas is a very moving play of the Christmas story put on by the Theatre Workshop, with accompaniment by the Community Chorus.

The Christmas Shoppers Stroll is a very popular event held every year on the first Saturday in December.

EPILOGUE

Nantucket is fragile, very fragile. The water table, the harbor, the marine life, and tourist activity—all must be cautiously weighed in the delicate balance between nature and people. The Island is so appealing and popular that the number of visitors increases each season, and measures to protect the Island's character have to be taken. That is why the chamber of commerce and others urge you not to bring your car if you're staying in the center of town. In January 1984, the Nantucket Land Bank, a plan designed to impose a 2 percent tax on all land transactions, was passed overwhelmingly. It is reputed to be the first in the country and is now copied by other communities. The proceeds from this tax are used to buy Island property for public use as part of an enormous effort by both native Islanders and summer residents to keep things in balance and leave land open.

It is difficult to even imagine what Nantucket would be like without the enormous contributions of time, money, land, and buildings by so many Islanders and summer residents. Because of their diligence and dedication, more than one-third of the Island is now preserved and protected from development, and fourteen buildings, owned and maintained by the Nantucket Historical Association, have been preserved for the public. It is a singular achievement; the resulting tracts of open land are now left to nature, to the rhythms of the seasons and the sea, just as they have been for centuries. These acquisitions of land and buildings have protected Nantucket's character and prevented her marshes and moors from being overrun with housing developments. The Conservation Foundation, the Massachusetts Audobon Society, the Maria Mitchell Association, the Nantucket Garden Club, the Trustees of Reservations, the Nantucket Island Land Bank Commission, the Nantucket Historical Association, the

Nantucket Land Bank, the Nantucket Land Council, and the Siasconset Trust welcome any contributions to help maintain this delicate balance between nature and man. In addition, Preservation Institute: Nantucket, which was founded by Walter Beinecke, Jr., and Professor Blair Reeves, is a summer college graduate program in architectural restoration studies. It has been very successful and beneficial to the town's unique historical preservation work.

It is very important for you, the visitor, to show as much consideration for the Island—which belongs to someone else—as if it were your own. You should realize you are an off-Islander from the "mainland" or "continent." Like all persons living on Islands, Nantucketers have a special pride and sense of place, an island consciousness with deep roots, which is, of

Sunset at Polpis Harbor.

course, one of the reasons for the Island's great attraction. Consideration of the Nantucketer's attitude, as you share the attributes of his home, is recommended for all visitors. There are many ways you can be helpful while you are enjoying your vacation: Leave your car on the mainland if possible; don't pick or dig up any wildflowers; leave all small shellfish entirely alone and encourage your children to do the same; do not trample the dunes and plant life growing on them; and, most important, do not leave any litter on the beaches.

The problem of preserving a bit of America's heritage was perhaps best expressed more than a century and a half ago when, in 1853, the beautiful sailing vessel *Young America* put to sea on her first voyage. Her famous shipbuilder, William H. Webb, turned to the ship's master and cautioned him, "Take good care of her, Mister. For when she's gone, there'll be no more like her."

When you visit Nantucket, take good care of her, for when she's gone, there'll be no more like her.

When you leave Nantucket, be sure to make a wish as you cruise past Brant Point Lighthouse. An old tradition is to throw two pennies overboard to ensure your return.

INDEX

Numbers in italics refer to pictures

A

accommodations, 49–69
    reservations, 3, 50–52
    service, 50–52
airplane
    instruction, 103
    to Nantucket, 37–38
Algonquian tribe. *See*
    Indians
Altar Rock, 168
ambulance, 88
American Seasons, 77
animal hospital, 88
Annual Arts Festival, 197
Annual Folk Art and Craft
    Show, 194
Annual Tree Fund Reception
    and Dinner Party, 194
antiques galleries, 94
antiques shows, 191–92, 193
apartments, 64–65
Arno's, 80
art galleries, 94
    instruction, 95
Artists Association, 95,
    183, 193
    art auctions, 95, *96,* 193
    crafts show, 194

astronomy, 95, 99–100, 105.
    See also Loines
    Observatory
Atheneum, 91, 99–100,
    125–26
auctions, 95, 193
automobiles
    bringing, vi, 33, 202
    on ferry, 33, 34–36
    rental, 34, 44–46
    sleeping in, vi–vii
    transportation to Cape
    Cod, 33

B

bakeries, 83
Baptist Church, *90,* 139
Barrett, John Wendell
    House, *118,* 129
Bartlett's produce farm, 177
beaches, 7, *10–11,* 96–98
    restrictions, vi–vii
Beachside Resort, 67
bed-and-breakfast accom-
    modations, 50–52, 60–65
Beinecke, Walter, Jr., 117,
    175, 203
berry picking, 98–99
bicycles
    race, 183
    rental, 44–46

About the Author

Polly Burroughs is a professional writer with a longtime understanding of island life. Formerly from Connecticut, she is now a year-round resident of Martha's Vineyard. She frequently visits nearby Nantucket, which she knows as intimately as her own island.

Her thirteen previous books include *Globe Pequot's Guide to Martha's Vineyard, Zeb: A Celebrated Schooner Life, The Great Ice Ship Bear, Thomas Hart Benton: A Portrait, Eisenstaedt: Martha's Vineyard, Martha's Vineyard Houses and Gardens* and *Alaska 1899,* with G.B. Grinnell and V. Wyatt.

When she's not writing, Mrs. Burroughs enjoys such island activities as tennis, swimming, and gardening.

Acknowledgments

The author is indebted to many organizations and individuals who have been extremely helpful in putting together the eighth edition of this guide. I am particularly grateful to Mimi Beman, owner of Mitchell's Bookstore; to Bob Taylor and Cary Hazelgrove; and to Frederick G. S. Clow for his wonderful photographs. A prize-winning photographer, Fred Clow was affiliated with the *Nantucket Inquirer and Mirror* for over thirty years, and he was a stringer photographer for United Press International for twenty-five years. His work has appeared in Time/Life Books, *Yankee* and *Smithsonian* magazines, and many other publications and newspapers. I'm also most fortunate to be able to include the work of Rob Benchley and Nicole Grant.

The late historian Charlie Sayle, Elizabeth Oldham, Dr. Wesley Tiffany, and the late Edward Stackpole were also most helpful on earlier editions. I'd also like to thank my editor, Christina Lester, for her fine suggestions.

Help Us Keep This Guide Up to Date

Every effort has been made by the author and editors to make this guide as accurate and useful as possible. However, many things can change after a guide is published—establishments close, phone numbers change, facilities come under new management, and so on.

We would love to hear from you concerning your experiences with this guide and how you feel it could be made better and be kept up to date. While we may not be able to respond to all comments and suggestions, we'll take them to heart and we'll also make certain to share them with the author. Please send your comments and suggestions to the following address:

The Globe Pequot Press
Reader Response/Editorial Department
P.O. Box 480
Guilford, CT 06437

Or you may e-mail us at:

editorial@globe-pequot.com

Thanks for the input, and happy travels!